The Reintegration
of Science
and Spirituality

The Reintegration of Science and Spirituality

The Reintegration
of Science
and Spirituality

Subtle Matter, Dark Matter
and Dark Energy

Deno Kazanis, Ph.D.

Styra Publications

The Reintegration of Science and Spirituality
Subtle Matter, Dark Matter, and Dark Energy

Published by:
Styra Publishers
6240 Greenwich Dr.
Tampa, FL 33647

ISBN 978-0-9717538-2-2
Spirituality
Science

Third Edition, 2013

TO MY WIFE BARBARA

AND MY SON PATRICK

The Reintegration of Science and Spirituality

The author presents a unique perspective by which science and spirituality can once again be integrated. By so doing he utilizes the philosophy and teachings of mysticism from all cultures, and the most recent developments in the physical sciences. The connection is simple and to the point, a connection which is likely to impact on all branches of science, without violating present systems of scientific development and knowledge. This will be of special interest to those who are seeking scientific connections, and those seeking experiential pathways of connection.

Deno Kazanis was born in Chicago and educated at the University of Illinois (B.S) and the University of Cincinnati (M.S.) in physics, and at The Pennsylvania State University (Ph.D.) in biophysics. He was also a Hargitt Fellow and Research Associate at Duke University for two years. In addition to his academic training, he has studied Tibetan Buddhism under Khenpo Konchog Gyaltsen of the Drikung Kagyu Lineage; Khenpo Karthar Rinpoche of the Karma Kagyu Lineage; Chogyam Trungpa Rinpoche of the Karma Kagyu Lineage; and Dr. Yeshi Donden, former physician to His Holiness the Dalai Lama. He has also studied Taoism under Master Mantak Chia of the Taoist Esoteric Yoga Center; Tai Chi Chuan under lineage students of Master Cheng Man-ch'ing; and Waidankung, an intense form of qigong from Taiwan, under lineage teachers. He also experienced Africa as a Peace Corps Volunteer in Nigeria and Kenya.

Acknowledgements

A deepest gratitude to all of the following individuals:

To my wife, Barbara Kazanis, for providing an environment which made this book possible, for providing numerous connections and resources for this book, for her patience, support understanding, and wisdom.

To those countless authors who I have referenced in this book who have done the footwork and paved the way for the world view presented in this book.

To my parents, my brothers and sisters, family and friends who have always supported my endeavors.

*"I have been in the heaven which takes most of his light,
And I have seen things which cannot be told,
Possibly, by anyone who comes down from up there;*

*Because, approaching the object of its desires,
Our intellect is so deeply absorbed
That memory cannot follow it all the way.*

*Nevertheless, what I was able to store up
Of that holy kingdom, in my mind,
Will now be the matter of my poem."*

--- Dante Alighieri, The Divine Comedy

*"Not only is the universe stranger than we think, it is stranger
than we CAN think."* – Werner Heisenberg

Brief Reviews

"Dr. Kazanis' book, *The Reintegration of Science and Spirituality*, has taken the complexity of science and made it clearly understandable. He has validated one's understanding of how prana (subtle energy) works as a source of energy. From the point of view of an instructor, the way he uses the concept of Koshas (subtle bodies), and multidimensional layers of the self, absolutely reinforces one understanding of how the natural process unfolds through attuning to the intelligence of the organism as foundation. This is a book every serious yoga practitioner and every yoga teacher must read." -
DON STAPLETON, Ph.D.
Co-Founder and Co-Director of the Nosara Yoga Institute, the Director of Interdisciplinary Yoga Teacher Training and author of *Self-Awakening Yoga.*

"Eventually modern science will have to come to terms with the issues raised by the great seers and mystics throughout history. Dr. Kazanis in *The Reintegration of Science and Spirituality*, has given us a bold, provocative look at how this synthesis may occur. -
LARRY DOSSEY, MD
Receiver of the prestigious Visionary Award, and author of numerous articles and nine books, including and *Healing Beyond the Body; Reinventing Medicine; Healing Words; Prayer is Good Medicine;* and *The Power of Premonitions*

"In his book, *The Reintegration of Science and Spirituality*, Dr. Deno Kazanis has clearly articulated an interesting hypothesis. **Something** is missing in contemporary physics, and it may turn out that dark matter solves cosmological puzzles, and even other puzzles we haven't yet defined." –
DEAN RADIN, Ph.D.
Chief Scientist at the Institute of Noetic Sciences (IONS), and author of *The Conscious Universe; Entangled Minds;* and *Supernormal.*

The Reintegration of Science and Spirituality offers a new and hopeful vision for the future. In a surprising manner, this book provides a basis in physics for mystical/spiritual phenomena. New discoveries from science regarding dark matter and dark energy are utilized to explain unanswered questions on the nature of paranormal phenomena, psychic phenomena, out-of-body experiences, near-death experiences, reincarnation, and a whole range of mystical phenomena. Dr. Deno Kazanis also presents an inspiring perspective on the traditional teachings and practices mankind has utilized to experience these phenomena.

Difficult concepts of science relevant to this discussion, are presented in a readable and concise manner bringing the reader in as a partner in inquiry as well as inviting one to give language and credibility to personal experiences that are easily shared with others.

Contents

V. PERSONAL ACCOUNTS

PREFACE

Years ago as I was practicing Tibetan meditations that involved the visualization of internal subtle structures of the human body (such as subtle channels and charkas), I began to realize that there must be a physical basis for these structures. But I could not imagine how since these structures were clearly not evident, and so I tucked that thought aside for the time being. Several years later I was reading an article on "dark matter," a dominant substance in the universe which is invisible. Due to my background in physics and my understandings of mystical teachings, by the time I had completed that article I understood how the subtle channels and charkas could be physical (have mass), could be invisible, and could exist within our visible body. This book is a detailed expansion and explanation of that insight, an attempt to show that what the mystics describe as the physical universe is very possible, and in fact, when all the evidence is weighed, it seems very certain.

In their book *The Soul, The Quality of Life*, Alice A. Bailey and Tibetan Master Djwhal Khul have stated, "The soul is as yet an unknown quantity. It has no real place in the theories of the academic and scientific investigators. It is unproven and regarded by even the more open-minded of the academicians as a possible hypothesis, but lacking demonstration. ... The [coming age] will see the fact of the soul demonstrated ... a discovery which will revolutionise, though not negate, the majority of their theories."[1] This book will show how modern science is unwittingly approaching this prediction and will soon provide a scientific basis for the soul, as well as scientific connections with the mystical/spiritual world.

It is hoped that, by providing a basis for the subtle bodies in physics, this book will point to the direction and methodology of exploration for the physical verification of the existence the subtle bodies as well as the soul, and intensify our understanding of what spirituality truly is about. Furthermore, a deeper understanding of traditional methodologies utilized throughout the history of humankind to directly experience these deeper, subtle aspects of our human nature, will be presented.

INTRODUCTION

"Aldous Huxley published a precious volume which he called The Perennial Philosophy and which is an anthology from the mystics of the most various periods and the most various peoples. Open it where you will and you find many beautiful utterances of a similar kind. You are struck by the miraculous agreement between humans of different races, different religions, knowing nothing about each other's existence, separated by centuries and millennia, and by the greatest distances that there are on our globe." – Erwin Schrödinger, Mind and Matter.

In our culture, many people have spiritual experiences but are unable to discuss them for various reasons. They may not wish to risk being ridiculed; they may have no language to convey the experiences; or they may have no scientific basis from which to explain them. While other cultures are very open to the exchange of such experiences, and give them considerable value, our society tends to marginalize them.

This book will be of interest to those who wish to ground their spiritual, psychic, or transforming experiences with a scientific understanding of the universe based in physics. It will enable others to open up to spiritual experiences, and enter into them. Spiritual and mystical concepts will be connected to scientific understandings of modern Western science in a meaningful and practical way. This will be done by focusing on two spiritual tenets common to mystical traditions of all cultures. On the one hand we will scientifically connect with the physical basis of mysticism by looking into the mystical belief that the universe consists of several "planes of matter" which are not visible to our normal vision, and show that the idea of subtle bodies made from these "planes of matter" is nearly universal outside of our culture. On the other hand we will look into traditional approaches to acquiring mystical experiences through the power of metaphorical processes; approaches for experiencing and developing awareness of the subtle bodies, which is a pathway to spiritual growth.[2]

It should be noted that mysticism contains a much broader range of topics than what could be covered in this book, and that there are numerous mystical doctrines from various cultures. Furthermore, this book does not contain all possible connections with the science of mysticism and subtle body theory. There are many more connections to be made, and we would encourage the reader to do so. This book will provide the first steps on a long and exciting journey.

We begin by noting that subtle body theory is coming increasingly into our view, perhaps because it can provide a physical basis for numerous phenomena which are presently unexplainable through Western science. At the heart of this we now find an increased public interest coupled with scientific explorations into phenomena such as subtle energies (qi, prana, ki, etc.), paranormal senses (clairvoyance, telepathy, telekinetics, remote viewing), psychic healing (hands on healing, healing through prayer), morphogenesis, geogenesis, cosmogenesis, near-death experiences, out-of-body experiences, reincarnation, to name a few. Accumulating scientific evidence has generated various models in an effort to account for each phenomenon independently. However, frontier scientists who are exploring these observable facts have disregarded the traditional comprehensive physical explanation which mysticism has provided for all of these and other related phenomena. We will explain how traditional mystical teachings assert that the creation of the universe is divided into several major planes of matter or consciousness, and that man, in addition to his visible body, has subtle bodies which interpenetrate with each other. Furthermore, we will discuss how these subtle bodies are composed of unique forms of matter made up from each of these planes, and how this is possible in terms of modern physics. These subtle bodies provide a logical and scientific explanation for all the phenomena listed, and more.

As we will see, when the mystics said that there are other "planes of matter" in the Universe which are invisible to our normal vision, that is exactly what they meant. Let us take a look at subtle bodies and the knowledge to which they will lead us.

CHAPTER I

THE PHYSICAL BASIS OF MYSTICISM

Subtle Bodies and Dark Matter

MYSTICISM

Mysticism is a discipline which explores, develops, accumulates and utilizes knowledge, concepts and techniques that are of spiritual value. It is a very pragmatic and elaborate discipline concerned with direct experience or awareness of spiritual truth, of ultimate reality, etc., which can be attained through immediate intuition, insight, or illumination. Mystical methodology is not based on external experimentation, but internal experience and observation. According to Lama Anagarika Govinda, "The mystic anatomy and physiology ... is not founded on the 'object-isolating' investigations of science, but on subjective – though not less unprejudiced – observations of inner processes, i.e., not on the dissection of dead bodies or on the external observation of the functions of human and animal organisms, but on the self-observation and on the direct experience of processes and sensations within one's body."[3]

Mysticism has a unique vocabulary for discussing states of mind that are encountered in one's spiritual development, but regards intellectual knowledge as only an aid to the direct experience of ultimate "truths," not as an "end in itself." This view can be contrasted with modern science, which is primarily an intellectual process quite suspicious and skeptical of direct knowledge through experience, and believes that ultimate truths are intellectually comprehensible, much like the laws of physics.

Mysticism has always maintained that humankind is composed of several subtle bodies made from various planes of matter. We will look into the feasibility of such a claim in terms of Western science.

SUBTLE BODIES

"When they are seen as fields of energy, human beings appear to be like fibers of light, like white cobwebs, very fine threads that circulate from the head to the toes. Thus to the eye of a seer, a man looks like an egg of circulating fibers. And his arms and legs are like luminous bristles, bursting out in all directions." A Separate Reality *by Carlos Castaneda*

The knowledge of subtle bodies is present in almost all cultures throughout the world and throughout time. As David Tansley says, "One of the most persistent beliefs held by man throughout the ages is that his physical form is but the reflection of a series of subtler bodies, and that in their totality these invisible, interpenetrating forms reflect the nature of God, the Cosmic Man crucified in space upon the cross of matter. Most, if not all, of the spiritual and philosophical writings and teachings that have emerged through the ages bear witness to this concept. It is clear that the ancient Egyptians, Chinese and Greeks, the Indians of North America, the tribes of Africa, the Polynesian Kahunas, the Incas, the early Christians, the Vedic seers of India, and the medieval alchemists and mystics of Europe, have all in one way or another seen man and the study of his anatomy, both physical and subtle, as a key to the nature of God and the universe."[4] Man has bodies visible and invisible. The subtle bodies are invisible to our normal vision but not invisible to our

2

subtle vision. The subtle bodies interpenetrate and interact with each other and with the visible body.

The subtle bodies and the "planes" of matter of which man and the universe are composed, comprises the physical basis for mysticism. As man opens to the more subtle aspects of his being, he can through his subtle bodies experience a world which corresponds to that particular subtle body.

There are numerous representations in many cultures, ancient and modern, of the subtle bodies. In India and Tibet, which perhaps provides the most systematic development of mystical teachings in the world today, we find the following description. Humankind is composed of several interpenetrating sheaths or subtle bodies called kosas, which are made up of matter from different planes, each of different relative density. The densest of these sheaths, the anna-maya-kosa, is what we normally regard as our physical body, the one that is visible to our normal vision, and which Western science has explored in great detail, down to its cellular and molecular behavior. The other sheaths, not regarded as being visible to our every day vision, are not recognized by Western science. The second sheath is a subtle, fine-material sheath called the prana-maya-kosa. Also known as the pranic or etheric body, this kosa gives the visible body life and consciousness through the prana.

The next even finer sheath is our "thought body" or "personality," called the mano-maya-kosa (mental body, see Figure 1). This body is necessary for rational and intellectual thinking. The fourth sheath is the body of our potential consciousness, named the vijnana-maya-kosa. Extending far beyond our active thoughts, it comprises the totality of our spiritual capacities and is apparently equivalent to the soul in Western mysticism. And finally we have the ananda-maya-kosa. "The last and finest sheath, which penetrates all previous ones, is the body of the highest, universal consciousness ...

3

(ananda-maya-kosa). It is only experienced in a state of enlightenment, or in the highest states of meditation (dhyana), and corresponds in the terminology of the Mahayana to the 'Body of Inspiration' or 'Body of Bliss.'"[5]

These sheaths are not separate layers, but are mutually interpenetrating, from the finest (the ananda-maya-kosa) down to the densest (our visible body). "The corresponding finer or subtler sheaths penetrate, and thus contain the grosser ones. Just as the material body is built up through nourishment, while being penetrated and kept alive by the vital forces of the prana, in the same way the body of active thought-consciousness penetrates the functions of *prana* and determines the form of bodily appearance."[6]

Mental body, pranic body, and visible body, however, are viewed as being penetrated and motivated by the still deeper and finer matter from which the material that our thought and imagination draws its substance, or is stored up. "It is therefore only the spiritual body ... which penetrates all the five layers and thus integrates all organs and faculties of the individual into one complete whole."[7]

As we go up the ladder of subtle bodies, the finer subtle bodies transcend and include the denser bodies. In mysticism the finest forms of matter appear to be associated with the deepest truths or spiritual understandings. It is said that matter is spirit in its densest form and spirit is matter in its most subtle form.

In Western mysticism, the subtle bodies are categorized somewhat differently. Very briefly, the first body is again the dense, visible body. Next, there is the etheric body (equivalent to the pranic body), followed by the astral body, which is the emotional body. The astral body is not specifically mentioned in the eastern system, but is apparently contained in the pranic body. Next we have the mental body, equivalent to the mano-maya-kosa. These first three bodies are not regarded as

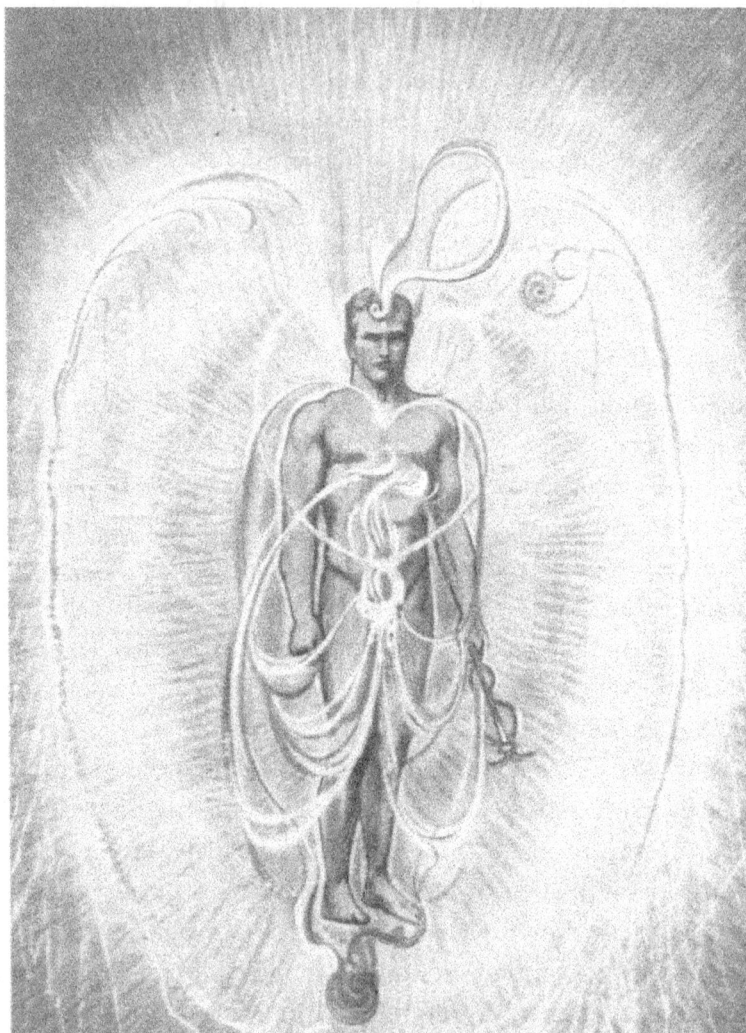

Figure 1. The Mental Body, Illustrated by M. from
The Dayspring of Youth, 1970, Yoga Publication Society

permanent, but as lasting for only one incarnation. Then there is the soul which is the vehicle of manifestation for the spirit and is veiled by these three bodies of mental, emotional and dense "visible" matter. Next is the causal body which contains the soul, and like the soul is relatively permanent, lasting many lifetimes. **It is the causal body and the soul which reincarnate in the process of our seeking our path back to the pure spirit.** The finest body is the "spirit" which can be thought of as being equivalent to the "body of bliss" in eastern systems, i.e. the ananda-maya-kosa.

But the subtle bodies have a complex anatomy and physiology of their own, and interact with each other as well as the visible body. The sheaths or mystical bodies contain the energy centers or charkas, which are also not visible to our normal vision. The chakras function by collecting, transforming and distributing the qi or prana. "From them radiate secondary streams of psychic force, comparable to the spokes of a wheel, the ribs of an umbrella, or the petals of a lotus. In other words, these chakras are at points in which 'psychic forces' and bodily functions merge into each other or penetrate each other."[8] Fritz Smith noted that, "The heretofore theoretical and abstract notions of the chakras became a reality for me as their form matched information I had learned in my study of Western medicine. These vortices of energy coincided with the curves of the skeleton."[9]

There are seven centers of psycho-cosmic force. The lowest of these is the Muladhara chakra (root-support), and is located, relative to the visible body, at the base of the spine (the sacral plexus). The next-higher one is called the Svadhisthana chakra. In Tibetan Buddhism, this center is usually not mentioned or regarded as an independent center, but is combined with the Muladhara chakra, under the name "sang-na," the "Secret Place." It corresponds to the sacral plexus, and stands for the whole realm of reproductive forces. The next center is at the solar plexus and is called the Manipura chakra (naval-lotus), and stands for the forces of transformation in the physical as well as in the psychic sense. The center that corresponds to the heart area is called the Anahata chakra, which regulates and controls the organs of respiration, just as the heart does. The three highest chakras are the Throat chakra or Visuddha (pure) chakra, corresponding to the plexus cervicus in the visible body; the Ajna (command) chakra, corresponding to the position between the eyebrows (the medulla oblongata); and the Crown chakra called Sahasrara-Padma, the "Thousand-petalled Lotus," which is associated with the pituitary gland in the visible body. In Tibetan Buddhism, the Ajna chakra is not separately mentioned, but is regarded as part of the Sahasrara-Padma or Crown chakra.

The connection between the subtle bodies and the chakras is not one-to-one. The anna-maya-kosa is primarily connected with the Muladhara, the Svadhisthana, and the Manipura chakras. The prana-maya-kosa is primarily connected with the Anahata and Visuddha chakras. The mano-maya-kosa and the vijnana-maya-kosa have the Ajna chakra as their center.

Connecting the sheaths (kosas) and chakras are subtle vessels called nadis, which serve as conductors of the energies that flow through the subtle bodies. To a certain extent, they parallel the nerve-system in the visible body, and they are very numerous. These subtle nerves make up the 12 acupuncture meridians (lung, large intestine, stomach, spleen, heart, small intestine, bladder, kidney, pericardium, triple warmer, gallbladder, liver) and the 8 extraordinary vessels (governing, conception, thrusting, girdle, yang heel, yin heel, yang linking, and yin linking). Of particular importance are the three major nadis: the susumna, the ida and the pingala. The central channel or susumna, runs like a hollow channel through the center of the spinal column, and the ida and pingala, are wrapped around the susumna-nadi in a spiral fashion, starting from the left and the right nostrils respectively, and meeting the susumna in the perineum at the base of the spine. They establish a direct connection among the seven chakras. In Tibetan descriptions, pingala and ida are often simply called the "right and left nadi," and there is no mention of a spiral movement of these nadis around the susumna.

Stanislav Grof notes that: "The patterns of energy flow in the subtle body described in the literature on Kundalini do not seem to be universal and absolute. In several instances, subjects who tuned into the Chinese archetypal world experienced the energy flow in a way that exactly followed the maps of meridians found in Chinese medicine and became aware of the special significance of the acupuncture points. This was followed by philosophical insights into the Chinese system of five elements (wood, fire, earth, water, and metal), which is distinctly different from the one found in the European tradition. I have also observed subjects who gained deep experiential understandings of the special role of the abdominal center (hara) and the dynamics of the ki energy underlying the Japanese martial arts."[10]

These subtle bodies and charkas and nadis composed of subtle matter are clearly quite different in nature from our visible bodies. And while our dense physical body requires external light to make them visible, the subtle bodies are self-luminous, having a radiant, clear glow about them. With our ordinary vision we cannot see these mystical subtle bodies, or the chakras, or the nadis, but with our subtle vision we can. And all these bodies and chakras interact with each other to form the whole human being. To function as a human being, we are constantly utilizing these subtle bodies even though we are not conscious of them. To the true practitioner of mysticism, these truths are as real as scientific truths are to the scientist. By turning inward, the mystics have concentrated their exploration of the universe on those concepts which are of value to spiritual growth.

But can Western science make sense of subtle matter and subtle bodies, and verify its reality? Is such matter possible? Can Western science confirm this age-old knowledge? To answer these questions we will next take a look at our present understanding of matter in Western science.

TABLE 1

SUBTLE BODIES FROM 3 CULTURES

India (5 bodies)	Western Mysticism (7 bodies)	Ancient Egypt (12 bodies)
1. Anna-maya-kosa (visible body)	1. Visible Body	**Material Realm** 1. Aufu (visible body)
2. Prana-maya-kosa (bears the universal life force, prana)	2. Etheric Body (receiver, assimilator and transmitter of qi or prana)	**Etheric Realm** 2. Sahu (the body of gold)
3. Mano-maya-kosa (cognitive mind)	3. Astral Body (emotional body)	3. Kahibit (the shadow or shade)
4. Vijnana-maya-kosa (discriminating intelligence, soul)	4. Mental Body (cognitive mind)	4. Khat (corporeal remains, of any form)
5. Ananda-maya-kosa (bliss-consciousness or body of joy)	5. Causal body (abstract mind, intuition)	**Mental Realm** 5. Ab (the heart of consciousness)
	6. Soul (pervades and holds the other bodies together as a cohesive, functional unit; reincarnates)	6. Ren (associated with words of power)
	7. Spirit (godhead)	7. Sekheim (magical power, will)
		Spirit Realm 8. Khu (divine intelligence)
		9. Ba (immortal soul)
		10. Ka (animating spirit)

TABLE 2. CHAKRAS

ABSORB AND TRANSFORM SUBTLE ENERGIES

CHAKRA	LOCATION	PROPERTIES
Sahasrara-Padme	Crown of Head	Throne of Spiritual Dominion "Thousand Petalled Lotus"
Ajna	Middle of forehead (third eye)	Universal Consciousness Gives inner vision
Visuddha	Throat	Spiritualized vibration of mentally and audibly formulated knowledge
Anahata	Heart	Intuitive Mind; spiritualized feelings; compassion, love
Manipura	Navel	Organ of transformation, equilibrium and assimilation
Svadhisthana	Sacral region	Personality
Muladhara	Base of spine	Physical experience; also habitat of Kundalini

FROM MATTER TO DARK MATTER

"It is high time now that scientists accept the existence of bioenergy (prana), the intelligent force behind all chemical actions and reactions of a biological organism. Here we deal with a new dimension of matter and consciousness. ... The experiments ... are yet in a rudimentary stage, but ... if the idea is based on a solid foundation, the experiments will be successful and the illusive medium will be located one day" --- *Gopi Krishna*, The Awakening of Kundalini

The concept of "planes of matter" as discussed in mysticism has been difficult to comprehend in terms of our seemingly advanced knowledge of matter in Western science. For that reason it hasn't been taken very seriously even by those individuals who are open to mystical teachings. However, the recent scientific discovery of dark matter in the universe has changed all that. Scientists chose the term dark matter because this matter can't be seen. As we will discover, this was an unfortunate name for this substance. Dark matter strongly suggests a true physical basis for subtle bodies and subtle "planes of matter" as described by the mystics. dark matter is the dominant substance in the universe, and is at least 10 times more prevalent than "luminous" or visible matter. "Dark matter is strange stuff. It's all around you but you can't see it. It's whistling by your ears but you can't hear it. It is arguably the most important material in the Universe, but until recently scientists had no idea it existed. ... How can scientists, after so many centuries, still know so little about the workings of the cosmos?"[11]

A Brief History of Matter

In order to more fully understand the connection of dark matter and the mystical concepts of "planes of matter" and subtle bodies, let us take a brief look at the development of the concept of matter by Western science.

In particular we need to understand the properties of "mass" and "electric charge." As we will see, normal matter, being made up of atoms, is composed of charged particles. All atoms have negatively charged electrons moving about a positively charged nucleus. At the atomic level, there is no such thing as "touch." When objects bump into each other it is the electric forces of the atoms that keep them from passing through each other. When atoms form molecules, it is their electric charge which is responsible for the formation of the molecules. Our vision, hearing, touching, etc., are all made possible because of electric charge. We will consider what would happen if there were "atoms" present in the universe which were not held together by electric charge, but some other "force."

Let us begin our history of physics with Newton's Laws of Motion. When Newton introduced "mass" in his Laws of Motion in 1687, he may well have believed that we saw and felt objects because of their mass. However, as science successfully explored the properties of matter, it became clear that the properties of mass had nothing to do with vision or sensation or the ability to hold objects. Mass was found to have just a few basic properties: (1) mass produces gravitational effects, as described in Newton's Law of Gravity; (2) mass has an inertial property, as described in Newton's laws of motion ($F=ma$; where F = force, m = mass, and a = acceleration); and (3) mass is a form of energy as shown by Einstein's Special Relativity in the 20th Century. In fact Einstein showed that an enormous amount of energy was required to produce a small amount of mass

13

($E=mc^2$; where E = energy, m = mass, and c = the speed of light). None of these properties of mass have anything to do with vision, or with the impenetrable boundaries of matter and our ability to see, feel, hear, taste or smell objects.

What became central to the behavior of physical matter were the properties of electric charge. Our understanding of electromagnetic phenomena was developed in the 19th century. First came the knowledge that electricity and magnetism were not independent phenomena, but related, when in 1819, Danish physicist Hans Christian Oersted discovered that an electric current (moving charge) could produce magnetism. In 1820 French scientist Andre Marie Ampere performed more precise investigations into the magnetic effects produced by current carrying wires, and also studied the forces between current carrying wires. Then in 1831 the English scientist Michael Faraday discovered that he could create an electric current in a conducting wire by moving a magnet near the wire (electromagnetic induction).

In the 1860's the complete picture of the interrelation of electricity and magnetism was scientifically described in Maxwell's Equations, which are the mathematical foundation of electromagnetic theory. In establishing these equations, James Clerk Maxwell discovered that **charge should be capable of producing electromagnetic waves**, and that the speed of these waves was the same as the speed of light, suggesting to Maxwell that **light was an electromagnetic wave.** This prediction was confirmed by Heinrich Hertz in 1888, who successfully produced radio waves with an oscillating electric current, just as Maxwell had predicted. Further investigations demonstrated what no one had imagined, that visible light was just a very small part of a much, much larger electromagnetic spectrum, which included electric waves, radio waves, microwaves, infrared radiation, visible light, ultraviolet light, x-rays, gamma rays and cosmic rays. But this also brought home a very fundamental understanding – **not only was electric charge responsible for electricity and magnetism, but electric charge was also responsible for light, i.e. vision, our ability to see.**

The 19th century also saw the exploration of the chemical elements. With some very important fundamental assumptions, such as atoms where the smallest indivisible particles of an element, and the atoms of one element could not change into the atoms of another element, the periodic table was developed and nearly completed by the end of the 19th Century. The universe was found to be simply composed of about 100 basic elements or atoms. At that time the universe was viewed as a steady state universe, with no beginning or end in time, and so these elements were viewed as always having been present, and not being composed of anything smaller. The valences of the elements were known, and therefore the chemical properties of atoms were thought to be "understood," even though it was not known "why" atoms had certain valences or what "basic force" was responsible for chemical reactions.

Toward the end of the 19th Century, J.J. Thompson discovered the electron, and it soon became clear that the electron was a part of the atom. Models of the atom were developed to accommodate this discovery. In 1898, J.J. Thompson proposed the "raisin-pudding" model, suggesting the atom was a positively charged sphere with electrons stuck to it like raisins in a pudding. This theory was consistent with classical mechanics but had no experimental evidence to support it, and explained nothing about the behavior of the atom. In 1911 Ernest Rutherford presented his model of the atom based on experiments performed on thin gold foil bombarded by alpha particles. His experiments suggested a dense positively charged nucleus surrounded by negatively charged electrons. Then in 1913, Neils Bohr proposed that the electrons orbit the nucleus of the atom in fixed orbits. He suggested that electrons emit or absorb energy in the form of light (quanta) when moving from one fixed-energy orbit to another. This model was consistent with Rutherford's model of the atom, and was valued because it explained the spectral lines of atoms.

After a hard fought battle with classical mechanics, a new picture of matter and the atom emerged in quantum mechanics. The theory is embodied by Erwin Schrödinger's Wave Equation, which he proposed in 1926. Amazingly, **the chemical properties of matter became attributable to electrical charge** (the same electrical charge found to be responsible for light in the previous century). The atom was found to be composed of low mass, negatively charged electrons moving about a very small but highly massive positively charged nucleus. The nucleus was so small that if it were the size of a grain of salt, the atom would be the size of a football field. The atom, from the point of view of the electric field, appears to be SOLID, but from the point of view of mass the atom appears to be very EMPTY.

Quantum mechanics showed that not only do we see objects because of electrical charge (and not because of the properties of mass), but we can hold and feel objects because of the properties of charge (and not because of the properties of mass). What prevents objects from inter-penetrating with each other is the electrical forces associated with each atom. It was the properties of charge on the atomic level that gave matter its boundaries, its apparent solidity both visually and tactilely. **In fact quantum mechanics showed that all of our senses, and therefore our entire experience with the outer world, is due to the property of electric charge. Particles lacking electric charge would be invisible, undetectable to any of our senses. And these uncharged particles could also pass right through our visible atoms – our visible world, because there would be**

no force to prevent their interpenetration. We will come back to these very basic issues shortly.

Dark Matter and Dark Energy

Dark Matter and Dark Energy: What are they? Maybe they're exotic, never-before-seen forms of matter and energy. Or maybe they reveal a hidden flaw in our understanding of how the universe works. But really the two terms are place holders for our abject ignorance. We could just as easily have labeled them 'Bert' and 'Ernie' or 'Without-a-Clue A' and 'Without-a-Clue B'.
Neil de Grasse Tyson

With quantum mechanics, the picture of matter appeared fairly complete. Science could now more deeply understand the behavior of atoms. Quantum mechanics became the basic principle in atomic physics, and basic principles have no deeper explanation for their truth, other than their ability to logically describe the behavior of matter.

As science pushed further into the subatomic properties of matter with high-energy physics, many new subatomic particles were discovered. However only the proton, electron, neutrino and photon were found to be stable particles in free space (i.e., do not decay into other particles). More recently, according to physicists' Standard Model, we find that neutrinos, along with particles like electrons and quarks, are regarded as the fundamental pieces of matter. The Standard Model is the theoretical picture that describes how the elementary particles are organized and how they interact with one another via the forces. It unifies the nuclear, electromagnetic, and weak forces and enumerates the fundamental building blocks of the universe. Today physicists view the universe as containing only five fundamental forces. Everything we experience is presumably due to these five forces (see Table 5).

However, that is still not the complete picture of matter. Presently, scientists have explored distant galaxies with highly sophisticated astronomical instruments, and have discovered and verified the existence of dark matter and "dark energy." Not only have they verified their existence, but they have also discovered that these two quantities are the dominant forms of energy/matter in the universe. According to the Planck space telescope, dark energy makes up 68.3% of the energy density of the universe, and dark matter makes up 26.8%, leaving "normal" matter making up just under 5%. (Normal matter refers to the matter in the universe we can identify, such all the as elements, all the stars, and neutrinos)

Dark matter is a general term referring to "unseen" matter in the universe that can only be detected indirectly (thus the term dark matter). Since dark matter can't be seen, astronomers determine its presence by observing its gravitational influence on visible objects such as galaxies. Because it has mass dark matter can exert a gravitational pull on visible matter. Also, mass can distort or bend light with its gravity (Einstein's General Relativity). This "gravitational lensing" can be subtle since gravity has a very weak influence upon light, and so the affect can require the analysis of detailed data on the images of thousands of galaxies. Astronomers have been able to detect gravitational distortions due to dark matter when viewing superclusters of galaxies stretching 10 million to 100 million light-years across the sky.

Dark energy is a hypothetical form of energy that permeates all of space is thought to be the reason for the accelerating expansion of the universe. The evidence for dark matter is indirect, but comes from observations which suggest the universe has expanded more in the last half of its life than in the first half.

So, looking into outer space with our most sophisticated instruments, we can observe gravitational influences on distant stars, gas clouds, nebulae, galaxies and other celestial phenomena, but we cannot see anything which produces these influences. "When you look out into the sky from planet Earth, you see lots of things – the Moon, other planets, the occasional comet and the stars of the Milky Way. In between these occasional solid bodies, we used to think, was the void. A little dust here, a little gas there. But basically emptiness. Well, the universe just doesn't look that way anymore. As seen by the modern astronomer, that space between the planets and stars is no longer empty, and it isn't just populated by the odd dust grain or elementary particle, either. It's filled with something called dark matter – something whose effects we can see, but whose distribution and identity we have yet to learn. ... Today, we understand that what we normally think of as the 'galaxy' – the pinwheel of stars – is in fact only a part of the entire structure. It is surrounded by, and immersed in, a globe of unseen 'dark matter' that makes up at least 80 percent of its mass. The real story of the Universe, it seems, is in its dark matter. "[12]

At this point, we will focus on dark matter. The exploration of dark matter has become a multidisciplinary effort involving physical cosmologists, particle physicists, astrophysicists, plasma physicists, and others. Predictions of what dark matter is falls into two broad categories, (a) large objects that do not emit much light, such as the remnants of burnt out stars (i.e. black holes and white dwarfs), or substellar objects (i.e. brown dwarfs or planets), or (b) small objects such as elementary particles which are **not** composed of charged particles and are therefore invisible (such as the neutrinos).

Scientists have determined that there is an enormous amount of invisible matter (or dark matter) in the "halos" of galaxies (the spherical area surrounding the luminous central disc of a galaxy). Leading researchers have found too few substellar objects, such as planets or brown dwarfs, to account for the huge mass in these halos. Similar investigations show that white dwarfs and other stellar remnants only account for a small percentage of what can't be seen in the galactic halo. This leads to the conclusion that most of the dark matter in the galactic halo is composed of a whole new kind of elementary particle or type of matter.

Physicists are pursuing the detection of particle dark matter with the expectation that this matter is predicted by one of the present models of physics: the Standard Model or some of its extensions such as the Peccei-Quinn Symmetry, Supersymmetry, Technicolor, or Superstring models, which predict particles, such as WIMPS (weakly interacting massive particles), or very light axions, heavy neutralinos, or other particles associated with these theories. In order to fit computer generated models of "dark matter," some scientists have suggested that dark matter must interact with itself through some unknown force. We feel that it is highly likely that an understanding of dark matter will transcend our present knowledge of the universe.

The physical distribution of dark matter in galaxies is different from visible "luminous" (ordinary) matter. The dust, gas and stars that make up the visible part of galaxies are concentrated is a flat, spiraling disk. On the other hand, dark matter is held out in a spherical halo around a galaxy. If dark matter were composed of charged particles, like "luminous" matter, then one would expect their distributions to be the same. One explanation for this difference is that dark matter is essentially dissipationless, and cannot cool (lose energy) by electromagnetic radiation. Since ordinary matter **is** composed of charged particles, it dissipates energy and falls further into the gravitational potential.

TABLE 3.   PROPERTIES OF CHARGE

1. Charges produces electric fields
2. Moving charges produce magnetic fields
3. Accelerating charges produce electromagnetic waves (light), and therefore charge is responsible for vision.
4. Quantum mechanics shows that charge is the binding force of atoms, holding electrons near the nucleus; charge is responsible for the behavior of atoms, their chemical properties, the reason objects feel solid, and the reason we can see objects.

TABLE 4.   PROPERTIES OF MASS

1. Gravitational Property   mass attracts mass

2. Inertial Property – mass resists acceleration, or a change in velocity:
    $F = ma$,   where
    F = force, m = mass, and a = acceleration

3. Mass is a form of energy,
    $E = mc^2$,   where
    E = energy, m = mass, and c = the speed of light

TABLE 5.

THE FIVE FUNDAMENTAL PHYSICAL FORCES

1. Gravity (mass); (long range, but weak)
2. Electromagnetic Force (charge); (long range)
3. Weak Nuclear Force (most elementary particles) (very short range, 10^{-17} m)
4. Strong Nuclear Force (nucleons) (very short range, 10^{-15} m)
5. Higgs Field (Higgs Boson)

TABLE 6.

THE DISTRIBUTION OF MASS/ENERGY IN THE UNIVERSE

1. Dark Energy ... 68.3%
2. Dark Matter ... 26.8%
3. Normal Matter ... 4.9%
    a. Free Helium ...4.0%
    b. Stars 0.5%
    c. Neutrinos, Heavy Elements ... 0.4%

Detailed explorations of the invisible dark matter in the halos of galaxies indicate that these spherically-shaped halos extend 1.5 million light-years from each galaxy's center and contain at least as much mass as 5 trillion suns. This exceeds the diameter of the visible portion of a galaxy by a factor of 10, and the mass by a factor of 1000. The dark matter of our Milky Way apparently extends out to connect with the dark matter of our nearest galactic neighbor, Andromeda.

But dark matter is not only found in the halos of galaxies, but between galaxies as well. The dark matter between galaxies can be mapped by taking advantage of the ability of gravity to bend light, (as predicted in Einstein's General Theory of Relativity). Light would normally travel in a straight line. However in the presence of gravity, even if that gravity is produced by an invisible source, the path of the light rays are deflected, producing skewed or distorted images of distant galaxies, when view from here on earth. This distortion can be utilized to determine the quantity and location of dark matter. High-resolution images of a small section of the sky were obtained by analyzing the distorted light observed from very distant galaxies. The information obtained by dark matter gravity distortions of these galactic images, were analyzed with the aid of state-of-the-art computerized imaging techniques. The distortion requires a statistical evaluation on many patches over the sky, which allowed an image of the intergalactic dark matter to be generated by the Canada-French-Hawaii-Telescope (CFHT) group. They showed that dark matter is concentrated into a web-like distribution of filaments that intersect at dense nodes. These images clearly show the overwhelming presence and importance of dark matter in the universe, even where no luminous or visible matter exists (see Figure 2). Furthermore, it is now believed that there are hundreds of invisible dark matter dwarf galaxies encircling our own Milky Way and other large visible galaxies. This evidence was also obtained through the so-called gravitational lensing techniques. These dark matter dwarf galaxies apparently contain few or no visible stars. All of this data truly alters our understanding of the universe.

Dark matter refers to any type of matter which is not readily detectable by ordinary astronomical observation, yet can produce a gravitational effect. The simple property of matter lacking charged particles would (1) make this matter invisible to our normal vision (and other senses), and (2) give matter the ability to interpenetrate or pass through visible or "luminous" matter (i.e. matter made up of charged particles, such as all the atoms of the periodic table). Although the existence of uncharged particles is not new, the discovery of dark matter seems different from what is known to date in that it makes up about 26.8% of the matter/energy in universe, and is apparently stable (does not decay into other particles). To get an idea of how massive dark matter is, there are about 200 billion stars in each of 170 billion galaxies. All the dark matter in the universe is estimated to be more than 50 times all those stars. This enormous mass of stable matter, apparently void of charged particles, presents a universe very different from that envisioned by scientists just a short time ago. It suggests something very new (or perhaps very old). Matter that is invisible and "interpenetrable" with visible matter strikes a chord with the subtle matter discussed by mystical traditions. They had insisted that most of the universe was invisible to our normal vision, and they were right. To clarify this connection, in the next section we will return to the subtle body and "planes of matter" concepts of mysticism.

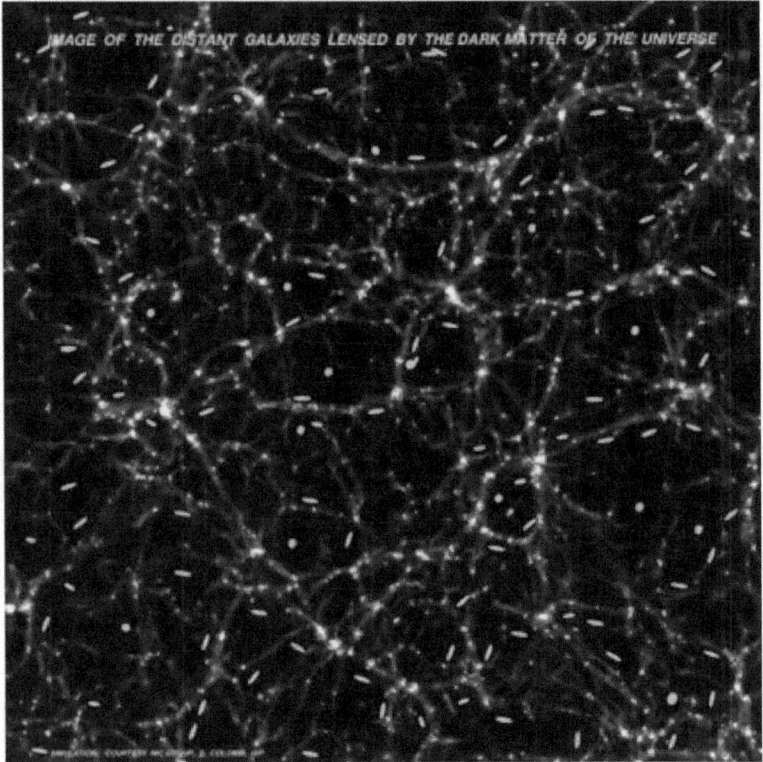

Figure 2. Distribution of Dark Matter in a Large Volume of the Universe.

The web like areas represent invisible dark matter. The small ovals are galaxies, which are also encased by dark matter. The gravitational distortion is quite small, and requires a careful statistical treatment on many patches over the sky.

These numerical simulations were kindly made available by CNRS/IAP/NIC/ S. Colombi & Y. Mellier.

TABLE 7

THREE POSSIBLE EXPLANATIONS FOR DARK MATTER

I. Large Massive Objects	II. Subatomic Particles	III. Subtle Matter (qi, prana)
A. Remnants from burned-out stars such as: 1. Black Holes 2. White Dwarfs B. Massive Compact Halo Objects (MACHOs), such as: 1. Brown Dwarfs 2. Large Planets	Elementary particles that do not have electrical charge such as: 1. Light neutrino 2. heavy neutralino 3. Very light axion 4. Weakly interacting massive particles (WIMPs)	Uncharged particles which can form "atoms" by interacting through a non-electromagnetic force. They compose the subtle bodies of life. What is commonly referred to as qi or prana.
Not Enough Found to account for dark matter	Some evidence for WIMPs has been found, but can it account for all dark matter?	We strongly suggest that this is the heart of what the dark matter in our universe is.

SCIENCE MEETS MYSTICISM

"When shamans enter nonordinary reality, the rules of the outer world are suspended. Horses fly, plants talk, fairies and leprechauns abound. Time as we know it is suspended. Shamans may, in ordinary time, spend half an hour journeying, but during that journey they may watch the sun rise and set. Outer rules of space are equally voided in these nonordinary worlds. With the aid of a spirit helper, great distances can be crossed in a moment or two of outer time."
– Sandra Ingerman, Soul Retrieval, Mending the Fragmented Self

Mystics have attempted to reveal to us the existence of invisible realms, but we could not understand how this could be so. However, with the scientific discovery that the dominant matter in the universe is indeed invisible (dark matter), this mystical understanding now seems very plausible. The picture fits together for reasons already discussed. According to our understanding of physics today, electrical charge is fundamental to light (electromagnetic waves), and electric charge is responsible for all of our senses, our vision, hearing, touch, taste, and smell. Charge is the force through which atoms interact, and thus prevents their interpenetrability. So, if we consider "matter" that is **not** composed of charged particles, this "matter" would be invisible to our ordinary vision (as well as undetectable by our other senses), and could also interpenetrate with visible matter. It would not be visible to our normal vision because our normal vision is dependent on light (electromagnetic waves) that is produced by charged particles. This matter could interpenetrate with visible matter because the electromagnetic forces would not repel or attract these uncharged objects. Two objects could exist in the same space at the same time, providing one was composed of uncharged particles, and the other was composed of charged particles. That is to say, there would be no force through which they could interact, and so they could interpenetrate. We know such uncharged matter does exist, such as neutrinos. However, if the universe contained "atoms" which were held together by a "force" other than the electromagnetic force, these "atoms" would not be visible to our normal vision and could interpenetrate with visible atoms. These invisible "atoms" could also form structures, such as "molecules," chakras, nadis, subtle bodies, in the same way that visible atoms can form molecules, organs, and our visible body.

This might not be more than good science fiction, except for two issues: (1) mystics have told us of matter which is invisible to our normal vision, and could interpenetrate with or pass through visible matter; and (2) scientists have recently discovered that at least 26.8% of the universe is composed of invisible energy/matter, referring to it as dark matter. (All the stars in the universe only make up about 0.5%).

According to mystics/shamans, our subtle bodies interpenetrate with our visible body and with each other. This would suggest that our various subtle bodies are composed of various forms of uncharged "dark matter," if they were to physically exist (have mass). Not being visible to our normal vision and being able to interpenetrate with visible matter are properties of matter lacking charged particles. What the mystics were describing was dark matter long before scientists discovered dark matter. How could they have known that such a matter could exist except by direct experience?

To the mystic who has acquired awareness of his subtle bodies and has thus acquired subtle vision, dark matter is not dark at all, but is in fact self-luminous, glowing from within. This vision is not dependent on electromagnetic waves, but "pranic" or "etheric" waves. In our everyday life we are unaware of the existence of our subtle bodies, but the true mystics have developed techniques which make it possible to experience the universe from the perspective of the subtle bodies. In so doing they can look out upon the world and observe the subtle dark matter with their corresponding dark matter subtle body vision.

Just as charge interacts with charge through the electromagnetic force, subtle dark matter would interact with subtle dark matter through a corresponding force (such as qi-force or pranic-force). The "light" produced by subtle dark matter is "pranic waves or light," analogous to the light produced by charged matter, electromagnetic waves.

Long before dark matter was discovered, C.W. Leadbeater said, "All these varieties of finer matter exist not only in the world without, but they exist in man also. He has not only the physical body which we see, but he has within him what we may describe as bodies appropriate to these various planes of nature, and consisting in each case of their matter."[13] Through our visible body we are able to experience the visible world. Similarly, through our different and unique types of subtle matter of which our subtle bodies are composed, man can experience the corresponding outer world when he becomes conscious of that subtle body and experiences the world through that respective subtle body. Again, Leadbeater says "The soul of man has not one body but many bodies, for when he is sufficiently evolved he is able to express himself on all these different levels of nature, and he is therefore provided with a suitable vehicle of matter belonging to each, and it is through these various vehicles that he is able to receive impressions from the world to which they correspond."[14]

From the point of view of physics, it would appear that what the mystics referred to as "planes of matter" would be matter held together by different binding forces. The matter we are most familiar with is bound together by the force of electric charge, and similarly other "planes of matter" would be bound together by other forces (such as qi or prana, mano, etc.).

What is also apparent is the following. Looking at the accounts of individuals who have experienced these other planes of matter (such as during near-death experiences or in mystical states), it would appear that the sense of time and space associated with these various forms of subtle matter are different from that associated with visible matter. Each subtle plane of matter seems to have a unique sense of time and space associated with it. This suggests that time-space relationships are dependent upon the type of matter one is conscious of, or is experiencing. Clearly this would make it very difficult to communicate these experiences to those familiar with only our usual sense of time and space.

It would appear that time and space are determined by the matter we are experiencing. We measure "space" by measuring matter – our spacial sense is dependent upon the spacial properties created by matter, and thus we perceive the dimensionality of "space" according to the dimensionality of matter we experience. Space puts no limits on matter, so our concept of space is an abstraction of the space created by matter. Similarly "time" is measured through the motion of matter. It is dependent upon matter for its measurement and experience, whether it's the rotation of the Earth or the movement of the hands of a clock. Space itself puts no limits upon either time or the spacial qualities of matter. Examples of descriptions of mystical impressions of these planes of matter might be found in the writings of Emanuel Swedenborg or Rudolf Steiner, or the art of Alex Gray, Lionel Feininger, and Salvador Dali, or the poetry of William Blake and William Butler Yates. Personal experience of such space-time experiences might be found in our dream states.

What scientists are calling dark matter today is made up of many ingredients. However the essence, the core, the heart of dark matter, is clearly subtle matter, the "planes of matter" which provide the physical basis of mysticism. In the next chapter, we will take a look at psychic and spiritual phenomena for which dark matter subtle bodies can provide a physical basis.

CHAPTER 2

SCIENTIFIC EVIDENCE FOR

SUBTLE BODIES

PRELIMINARY REMARKS

The existence of other "planes of matter," and the subtle bodies with their charkas and nadis, provides a strong theoretical basis for numerous phenomena such as qi (ki, prana), out-of-body experiences, near-death experiences, clairvoyance, energy healing through touch and prayer, reincarnation, morphogenesis, cosmogenesis, etc. An exploration of these phenomena provides very convincing evidence for the existence of subtle bodies, and that the universe includes enormously more than that which comes within the range of ordinary vision and present day science. Furthermore, a dark matter subtle body theory can shed light and provide possible insights into numerous other spiritual issues. It may open one to transpersonal/spiritual experiences, or help one to understand and accept such experiences. It can provide a roadmap for spiritual stages and spiritual growth. Let us take a more careful look at some of these phenomena.

SUBTLE ENERGY

The concept of a subtle energy, or qi, appears to be universal. It is regarded as the primordial life force itself, and is given different names by different cultures (see Table 8).

It should be noted that the use of words such as "qi" can cover a lot of territory. The term "qi" can apply to these various levels of subtle matter, or to the binding or transmitting energy associated with the different levels of subtle matter. It would be as if Western science referred to all electromagnetic phenomena, including chemistry, simply as "charge." Mystical teachings have not analyzed subtle matter in the same way Western science has analyzed our "charged" matter. This analysis and categorization will be left to Western scientists.

How real is subtle energy? To those who have explored it, it is very real and easily detectable. There is an "International Society for the Study of Subtle Energies & Energy Medicine," and they produce a Journal entitled "Subtle Energies," which publishes many articles on the exploration and verification of subtle energies. Today you can find "many published reports of experiments in which persons were able to influence a variety of cellular and other biological systems through mental means. The target for these investigations have included bacteria, yeast, fungi, mobile algae, plants, protozoa, larvae, insects, chicks, mice, rats, gerbils, cats, dogs, and well as cellular preparations (blood cells, neurons, cancer cells) and enzyme activities. In human 'target persons,' eye movements, muscular movements, electrodermal activity, plethysmographic activity, respiration and brain rhythms have been affected through direct mental influence."[15] However, Western science cannot precisely say what subtle energies are, cannot specify the mechanism of subtle energies, and cannot credit a given therapeutic result to subtle energies with certainty. A functioning model for this phenomena has not been developed. Yet it seems clear that the best model for subtle energy phenomena, that of subtle bodies, has been overlooked, perhaps because we can't readily see these bodies, and so we don't take them seriously.

Subtle energy, or qi, has both local and nonlocal effects and is associated with prevention of disease, healing, the martial arts, as well as spiritual growth. In Esoteric Taoism, circulation of qi along pathways inside the subtle bodies is capable of producing improvements in health and life, and there are many methods of circulating qi, from acupuncture/acupressure, to specialized movements (qi-gong, tai chi), to visualization and meditation. Through Taoist techniques one can attract external qi in through the chakras. In Kriya Yoga, prana can be developed through asanas (postures), mudras (gestures), mantras (seed-sound syllables), and bandhas (muscular contractions). Qi or prana has properties that are not explainable in terms of physical matter as we know it. Although some have suggested that qi is a form of electromagnetic energy, it would have been all too easily detectable if this were so. Furthermore, this would require an entire electromagnetic information transmitting system, and a complete information receiving and interpreting system, which living systems do not seem to have.

Traditionally, prana is associated with the subtle body called the prana-maya-kosa. The failure of the west to verify such a subtle body has led to alternative models about qi or prana. Suggestions such as "bio-fields" or "morphogenic fields" have been made. However, in physics, "fields" do not exist independent of matter. According to the Standard Model, forces are communicated between particles by the exchange of quanta which behave like particles. You cannot have "fields" produced by non-matter, or independent of matter. To postulate new

33

physical "fields" is to postulate new physical matter. To postulate non-physical "fields" is physically meaningless. For example, electromagnetic fields are produced by charge, and nuclear fields by nucleons, and gravitational fields are produced by mass; or in terms of the Standard Model, electromagnetic phenomena involves charges exchanging photons, and the nuclear force involves nucleons exchanging gluons. "Bio-fields" or "morphogenic fields" may seem to have meaning, but do not provide a true physical explanation.

With the understanding that "dark subtle matter" (pranic matter) makes up the prana-maya-kosa, it would appear that qi or prana is simply a form of "dark matter," and there must be a quanta of "dark energy" transmitted by qi-dark matter. The term "qi" or "prana" as normally used seems to apply to both the particle and the quanta exchanged. Up to now, it has been extremely difficult to establish a physical basis for subtle bodies because we simply did not know what to look for, and it was difficult to accept them as physically real. Furthermore, subtle dark matter does not readily interact with visible matter, and so detection would have been very difficult, at best. Utilizing the knowledge that the subtle bodies have a dark matter physicality, we can provide a basis here-to-fore unattainable. Furthermore, we know direct interactions between subtle bodies composed of pranic matter is quite possible, and skilled practitioners of qi or prana have perfected techniques which enable them to transmit this energy externally. Qi can also affect the subtle bodies by entering through the chakras and being transmitted through the body by the nadis, in turn affecting the visible body.

However, we should be aware that the properties of qi or prana cannot be completely reduced to the same laws of physics which govern visible matter. After all, qi is regarded as being the "life force" and has additional properties which take it out of the limited behavior of the relatively dead matter of the visible world, and in fact gives our charged, visible matter its animation. One could perhaps say that the physical laws governing visible matter are a *special case* of subtle dark matter.

Quite possibly "cold fusion" is a form of subtle energy which can be accounted for by dark matter. Pons and Fleischmann used the term "cold fusion" for their unique energy generating discovery, because the energy that was produced was too great for a chemical reaction and so they thought it must be nuclear, but there was no radioactivity. Therefore they referred to it as "cold fusion." This phenomenon was met with enormous skepticism, particularly by nuclear physicists in the USA. However, recent scientific and commercial developments in cold fusion seem to confirm their discovery. Dozens of laboratories have replicated this work, and the results have been published in scientific journals. These developments seem to vindicate Pons and Fleischmann and may yet lead to a breakthrough in cold fusion as practical energy source. Is it nuclear or is it chemical? Since subtle dark matter is ever present, and since dense physical matter must interact with pranic "dark matter," Pons and Fleischmann may have come across a mechanism which allows the interaction between these two types of matter, and thus generating energy. In this way we could have a strong energy source, but no radioactivity, by utilizing "subtle dark matter."

TABLE 8

CULTURAL TERMS FOR SUBTLE ENERGIES [*]

Term	Culture
Ankh	Ancient Egypt
Arunquiltha	Australian aborigines
Gana	South America
Ki	Japan
Mana	Polynesia
Manitou	Algonquia
M'gbe	Hiru pygmy
Mulungu	Ghana
Ntoro	Ashanti
Ntu	Bantu
Oki	Huron
Orenda	Iroquois
Pneuma	Ancient Greece
Prana	India
Qi	China
Sila	Inuit
Tane	Hawaii
Ton	Dakota
Wakan	Lakota

---

[*] Taken from *Alternative Medicine, Expanding Medical Horizons,* NIH Publication No. 94-066, December 1994

ALTERNATIVE METHODS OF HEALING

There is a large body of research which supports both local and nonlocal energy based alternative therapies, such as spiritual and psychic healing, hands on healing techniques (biofield), and oriental medicine techniques such as acupuncture/acupressure. These methods have been so successful that they have attracted large numbers of individual to their doors, and the public has demanded research into these disciplines. Today, the National Institute of Health has a Department of Alternative and Complementary Therapies, to study, inform and provide grants for research. Numerous models have been proposed to explain these phenomena. In view of our understanding of subtle dark matter and the knowledge of the subtle bodies of mysticism, let us see what insights the combining of science and mysticism sheds on the process by which these alternative therapies operate.

Let us take a look at some of these alternative methods of healing.

Laying-on of Hands

Energy healing or the laying-on of hands is an ageless tradition of therapy. It is believed to operate directly by transferring healing energy from one person to another. Most practitioners believe that this biofield extends outward from the body, so actual touching of the visible body is unnecessary. They also believe that it is energized by an energy source which they mediate. Clearly we are dealing here with the dark matter etheric and/or astral subtle bodies. This qi energy can affect the subtle bodies through the meridians or the chakras. The visible physical body can in turn be easily affected through the subtle bodies.

This dark matter subtle body explanation for qi can also implement a basis for essentially all biofield therapies and therefore provide and satisfy the desired scientific basis. The role of the etheric body is to "act as a receiver, assimilator, and transmitter of prana."[16] Thus the subtle bodies may supply a simple and direct way for healing via the prana-maya-kosa. A healing touch would presumably allow the qi or prana in that corresponding subtle body of the patient to flow properly, which in turn can have beneficial effects on the visible body.

Acupuncture/Acupressure

According to the classical Chinese explanation for acupuncture, subtle energy runs through 12 channels or meridians in the body. These meridians are named according to the organs they primarily affect (lung, large intestine, stomach, spleen, heart, small intestine, bladder, kidney, pericardium, triple warmer, gallbladder, liver). There are also eight strange or mysterious qi vessels (governing, conception, thrusting, girdle, yang heel, yin heel, yang linking, and yin linking) which are connected to the meridians and share the function of circulating the qi throughout the body. The application of needles to certain acupuncture points which lie along these channels, has been shown to stimulate the body to release chemicals. The increase of endogenous opiate production, of substances that change the pain threshold, of substances that change the receptor sensitivity to the brain and in the nerve have been verified. In certain circumstances acupuncture has been shown to induce the production of a substance P which is a nerve growth factor. It is difficult to understand why needles should have any effect on the production of chemicals, or affect the organs, muscles, spinal cord or brain (and only stimulation at specific points in the human body). Although acupuncture/acupressure techniques make little sense in terms of Western physiology, they do make sense in terms of subtle body physiology. If we consider the nadis or nerves of the subtle bodies, the acupuncture/acupressure points become the points where the dense physical (visible) body connects with or binds to the etheric (pranic) body. Thus by stimulating these points we are stimulating the etheric (pranic) body, in particular the nadis in this subtle body, which in turn can affect the entire subtle body, which in turn affects the organs of the visible body. Thus the stimulation of biochemicals with needles becomes more understandable.

Even healing techniques, where there is physical manipulation of the body, such as massage, chiropractic therapies and others, can create a balancing of the qi energy flow through the nadis or chakras. And because the major chakras are located along the spine and in the cranium, these chakras can be significantly affected by spinal manipulation and cranial-sacral therapies – even when the manipulation is very gentle, since the hands are immersed in the pranic/etheric or astral body of the client.

Qigong

"For hundreds of years Westerners have been puzzled at seeing Chinese from all walks of life doing this effortless, rhythmical, ballet-like exercise both at dawn and at dusk. By way of explanation, Chinese say that whoever practices Tai Chi, correctly and regularly, ... over a period of time will gain the pliability of a child, the health of a lumberjack, and the peace of mind of a sage." Cheng Man-ch'ing.

Qigong literally means "qi cultivation," and refers to a family of exercises developed in China over a few thousand years. There are literally thousands of forms of qigong. Tai Chi Chuan is a form of qigong based on martial arts movements. A detailed review of the basis of qigong and techniques would be another book entirely.

But in general, qigong is a sophisticated exercise system which, if practiced regularly, is regarded by the Chinese to have numerous benefits, such as (1) relieving disease states, and promoting general health, (2) increasing vitality, (3) mobilizing the muscles and joints and improving flexibility and balance, (4) increasing the sharpness of the senses, (5) enhancing concentration and memory, (6) activating the qi in the body, as an acupuncture treatment would, (7) engaging the physical, mental, emotional, and spiritual levels of the individual, (8) stimulating latent parapsychological abilities, and (9) prolonging life. Some of these effects have been shown to be true, and none have been disproven. Research in China has shown countless benefits, both short term and long term, and Western science continues to be amazed that the slow and gentle movements of many forms of the qigong have been shown to have beneficial effects on nearly every physiological measurement that can be made. Again, difficult to comprehend from the point of view of Western medicine, but the internal energy developed in qigong is subtle body energy (qi), and qigong, with is ritualistic movements, simply provides a slow but effective way into a direct utilization and an awareness of the subtle bodies. Qigong is a methodology which connects with and positively activates the subtle bodies, and in turn the visible body.

Yoga

Indian Yoga can make claims similar to those of qigong. The Yogic postures (asanas) also work on a subtle body system, often leading to the release of the kundalini – a very special subtle body energy. Grof notes, "Another interesting group of phenomena is related to the concept of the Serpent Power, or *Kundalini,* which plays an important role in the Indian spiritual tradition. According to the Hindu and Buddhist Tantric schools,

Kundalini is seen as the creative energy of the universe that is feminine in nature. In her external aspect, she is manifested in the phenomenal world. In her internal aspect, she lies dormant at the base of the human spine. In this form, she is traditionally symbolically represented as a coiled serpent. Activated by spiritual practice, by contact with a guru, or spontaneously, it rises in the form of active energy, or Shakti, up the conduits in the subtle body called nadis, opening and lighting up the psychic centers, or charkas.

"Although the concept of Kundalini found its most elaborate expression in India, important parallels exist in many cultures and religious groups – in the Taoist yoga, Korean Zen, Tibetan Vajrayana, Sufism, the freemasonic tradition, the !Kung Bushman of the African Kalahari Desert, North American Indian tribes, especially the Hopi, and many others."[17]

Kundalini forms the basis of all yogic disciplines, representing the female energy in latent form and containing the vast potential of psychic energy. The objective is to awaken the cosmic energy and cause it to unite with the Pure Consciousness which pervades the entire universe. This process usually involves considerable discipline and extensive training, but practices vary considerably. Typically practices involve yogic breathing techniques, asanas, mudras, mantras, and bandhas.

However, the arousal actually takes place in the subtle bodies. When the Kundalini is aroused she ascends through the susumna (the central channel) and passes through all the chakras that lie along the axis of the spine as consciousness potentials, and unites above the crown of the head with Pure Consciousness. The ascent of Kundalini as it progresses through the chakras, manifests physical and psychic signs. Preceding the arousal, the body may tremble, and as the kundalini progresses through the chakras, intense heat may be experienced, and the part where the kundalini is passing can be burning hot. Inner sounds are usually heard, resembling a waterfall, the sound of a bell, a flute, etc. There may be tingling sensations in the spinal cord and/or all over the body; there may be involuntary laughing or crying; one may see visions of deities or saints. Dream-scenes of all kinds may appear, from the heavenly to the demonic. One may experience prana flowing in the brain or spinal cord. Spontaneous chanting of mantras or songs may occur.[18]

Prayer and Mental Healing

There is considerable scientific evidence for the healing power of prayer and its effectiveness in medicine, as shown by Dr. Larry Dossey. However, Dossey also points out that, "We simply don't know how the mind of one person can engage in 'action at a distance' to bring about the healthful changes. ... Conventional forms of energy are an insufficient explanation for what we observe in spiritual healing experiments. In them the 'energy' does not fade away with increasing distance, and it cannot be shielded, as we would expect if ordinary forms of energy were involved."[19]

Clearly dark matter and subtle body theory could present a simple explanation, since dark matter is void of charged particles it would be essentially unaffected by visible matter. Energy in the form of thought could be transmitted by the mano-maya-kosa of one person and received by the mano-maya-kosa of another person. This mental body is believed to be capable of transmitting thoughts from one mental body to another. Normally we are not aware of these thoughts, but if one is conscious of the mano-maya-kosa, one can perceive these thoughts. The energy transmitted on this level of fine matter would not only be unaffected by visible matter, but the space-time relationships associated with the matter of the mano-maya-kosa are so different, that our normal sense of distance would be irrelevant. These thoughts (energy) received by the mano-maya-kosa or the charkas could in turn effect the gray matter of the brain and stimulate action on the psycho-neuro-endocrine pathway or the psycho-neuro-immunological pathway. Psychic energy can enter through the chakras as well. The subtle body model elegantly accounts for nonlocal spiritual and psychic healing.

The Placebo Effect and Spontaneous Remission

The ability of an "inert" substance to have a curative effect on an individual is well documented. In early contemporary scientific medicine, if a patient was cured by a non-pharmaceutical substance, such as sugar, while being told it was medicine, it was usually assumed that the individual did not have the illness to begin with (it was in their head). However, that doesn't hold up any more. Individuals with documented illnesses have improved their condition by taking a placebo. This effect is so common that in order to test the effectiveness of a pharmaceutical drug, one must eliminate the placebo effect. This is best done with double blind, randomized, placebo controlled trials. This involves giving the actual drug to one group and the placebo to another group, with neither the patients nor those administering the drug aware of who gets the placebo and who gets the actual drug. At the end of the trial the results are compared to see if the drug is significantly more effective than the placebo. Although the placebo effect is an accepted phenomena in medical science, there is no understanding of the mechanism by which it operates. In 1975, Benson and Epstein remarked, "should not the placebo effect be further investigated so that we might better explain its worthwhile consequences?"[20]

However, the scientific community has treated the placebo effect as a nuisance because it gets in the way of testing "real" medicine. As a result the mechanism of the placebo has not been scientifically researched. Rather than trying to maximize the placebo effect, science would like to eliminate it. So we don't know if the placebo effect is influenced by taste, smell, color or anything else. It's quite possible that for certain ailments, a bitter taste might be more effective, and for others a sour taste, in some cases red, others green, but this really hasn't been scientifically explored. In truth, the placebo effect is potentially an ideal cure with no side effects.

It has been observed that in testing some therapeutic drugs, that although the drug was effective in most parts of the world, in some countries it did not pass the double blind, randomized, placebo controlled trials. Not because the effects of the drug were diminished in that country, but because the placebo effect was so high. For example when testing the H2 blocker cimetidine, 31 trials were performed in different countries. The drug proved to be very effective in all countries except in Germany where all 4 trials failed because the placebo effect was so high.[21] This is obviously not the case for all medicines tested in Germany.

Related to the placebo effect is spontaneously remission, which is the disappearance of an illness for no apparent reason. Why someone who is apparently dying of cancer, for example, should suddenly recover without therapy is even more difficult to explore than the placebo effect, but they seem to have something in common.

From the point of view of the dense physical body, our traditional understanding of anatomy and physiology, these effects are puzzling. But from the point of view of the subtle body, there are numerous reasons as to why the curative powers of the etheric/pranic body or even the mental body might be stimulated and produce a healing effect on the dense physical body of an individual.

EXTRASENSORY PERCEPTION AND PARANORMAL PHENOMENA

"The effects observed in a thousand psi experiments are not due to chance, selective reporting, variations in experimental quality, or design flaws. They've been independently replicated by competent, conventionally trained scientists at well-known academic, industrial, and government-supported laboratories worldwide for more than a century, and the effects are consistent with human experiences reported throughout history and across cultures."
Dean Radin – The Conscious Universe

Paranormal phenomena includes a broad category of experiences such as telepathy, clairvoyance, psychokinesis, precognition, remote viewing, premonition, levitation, etc. These phenomena suggest the presence of a non-visible interaction among people, objects and events, and makes it clear that our present understanding of the universe is incomplete in fundamental ways.

We find considerable skepticism among many mainstream scientists who wish to believe that psychic phenomena is a combination of delusions, or misperceptions, or wishful thinking, fraud, etc. They are aided by the reality that some psychic phenomena is actually fraud, or delusion, or fantasy. However, the book *The Conscious Universe* by Dean Radin, provides a comprehensive summary of our present status in parapsychology. Clearly, there is now persuasive scientific evidence for psychic phenomena, particularly evidence that has been produced over the last 50 years by reputable scientists around the world who have established that some psychic phenomena are real.

Clairvoyance, however, is not limited to humans. In 1966, Cleve Backster, an expert lie-detector examiner, connected, out of curiosity, his lie detector to the leaf of a dracaena (also known as the dragon tree). This began an unexpected adventure, which is described (along with many other related phenomena) in the book, *The Secret Life of Plants: A Fascinating Account of the Physical, Emotional, and Spiritual Relations Between Plants and Man.* Before Backster was through, he discovered that the plants reacted to thoughts. He discovered their reaction could occur at some distance, and even discovered by synchronizing time with his lie detector, that plants reacted to events, such as when he <u>thought</u> about coming home. "But he had no idea what kind of energy wave may carry man's thoughts or internal feelings to a plant. He has tried to screen a plant by placing it in a Faraday cage as well as a lead container. Neither shield appeared in any way to block or jam the communication channel linking the plant to the human being. The carrier-wave equivalent, whatever it might be, Backster concluded, must somehow operate beyond the electromagnetic spectrum."[22] This is the same conclusion reached by Dr. Larry Dossey in his experiments on the power of prayer, and also the same conclusion reached by researchers on subtle energy phenomena in general.

Similar results have been obtained in working with the animal world. Biological experiments have shown an interaction which occurs between living organisms which also cannot be accounted for with our present understanding of physics. Using synchronized filming, Rupert Sheldrake demonstrated that dogs left at home will noticeably respond when their masters <u>think</u> about coming home.

Of recent interest is the phenomena of remote viewing (RV). "Remote viewing is a mental faculty that allows a perceiver (a 'viewer') to describe or give details about a target that is hidden from normal senses due to distance, time, or shielding. For example, a viewer might be asked to describe a location on the other side of the world, which he or she has never visited; or describe an event that happened long ago; or perceive an object sealed in a container or locked in a room; or perhaps even describe a person or an activity; all without being told anything about the target – not even its name or designation. ... And the sorts of targets used for RV research differed from those typically found in other psi research. Targets chosen for 'viewing' included geographic locations, hidden objects, and even such things as archaeological sites and space objects about which it was expected that ground truth would soon be known, so that the viewer's accuracy could be checked.

... Some RV theorists think that formal RV methods are really just strategies that help the viewer to more successfully and reliably access his or her own subconscious mind, where many believe information obtained from RV first emerges into human consciousness."[23]

The declassification of a 25 year RV training program by the CIA has given remote viewing credibility, and generated great interest nationally and internationally.

A physical model for the explanation of RV has not been put forth, but again we find that the subtle body doctrine provides an explanation for these phenomena, and suggests that remote viewing techniques tap the knowledge obtained through the subtle bodies. As mentioned, the mental body (or mano-maya-kosa) is capable of transmitting thoughts from one mental body to another. If we have a physical subtle dark matter mano-maya-kosas, clairvoyance is a distinct possibility. As C.W. Leadbeater puts it, "In man's physical body there is etheric matter as well as solid matter which is visible to us ... and this etheric matter is readily visible to the clairvoyant. In the same way a more highly developed clairvoyant, who is capable of perceiving the more refined astral matter, sees the man represented at that level by a mass of that matter, which is in reality his body or vehicle as regards that plane; and exactly the same thing is true with regard to the mental plane in its turn. ... Every time that we think, we set in motion the mental matter within us, and a thought is clearly visible to a clairvoyant as a vibration in the matter, set up first of all within the man, and then affecting matter of the same degree of density in the world around him. But before this thought can be effective on the [dense] physical plane it has to be transferred from that mental matter into astral matter; and when it has excited similar vibrations in that, the astral matter in its turn affects the etheric matter, creating sympathetic vibrations in it; and that in turn acts upon the denser physical matter, the gray matter of the brain."[24]

It would appear that plants and animals have a more basic connection with their subtle bodies and can more easily pick up on these signals. We, on the other hand, have relegated this connection to our unconscious.

We know from spiritual teachings that psychic powers *(siddhi)* are often part of the spiritual path. "For Buddha, as well as for Pantajali, the *siddhi* are *paranormal powers the possession of which cannot be avoided.* In the course of their ascetic and contemplative labors the yogi and the *bhikku* necessarily come to a plane of experience on which extra-sensory experience and all the other 'wonderful powers' are given to them. Buddha, Patanjali and others drew attention not only to the danger of 'exhibiting' such 'marvelous powers' but to the dangers that they present to their possessor; for the yogi is in danger of yielding to the temptation of magic; being content to enjoy the marvelous powers instead of sticking to his spiritual work and obtaining the final liberation."[25]

DIVINING

Although divination is given little importance today in the Western world, cultures throughout the world and throughout time have utilized divining for a multiplicity of purposes, from finding food and water, to curing illnesses. "Divining is as old as humanity. The hunters developed it as a ritual to discover the location of game, a matter of vital importance to them. As other types of societies arose, divination was adapted to the changing circumstances, but it continued to serve important societal goals. It is regrettable that in the Western world divination has been decried as irrational, antirational, or a fraud perpetrated on the ignorant and the superstitious, because divination is not that at all."[26]

Numerous devices are utilized to aid the diviner in this practice, such as rods, bones, bowls, sticks, stones, cards, postures, etc. True divining is utilized primarily for societal good, and is distinguishable from "fortune telling."

Once again, we find that the subtle bodies are at the heart of this process, and can provide a physical basis for these phenomena.

ASTROLOGY

Astrology is an ancient science still utilized by many modern world cultures. In the not too distant past, astrology and astronomy were united. At that time the interest in astronomy and the accurate measurement of the movement of heavenly bodies was of value because it enabled more precise astrological information.

It should be noted that astrology frequently plays a more fundamental in non-western cultures.

"When a male child is born in the West, the parents, if they can afford it, take out insurance for his education. They have him immunized and inoculated and put his name down for a good 'school.' Twice a year they take him to a dentist. But they do not attempt to arrange his marriage, nor, when he reaches puberty, do they solemnly and with fearful ceremony initiate him into mysteries of sex and his male role in life.

"It is not so elsewhere. In Asia the precise moment of his birth is carefully noted so that the astrologer may prepare his horoscope. And throughout his life this horoscope will be closely consulted at every step he takes, most particularly in regard to his marriage, which will have been planned for him at the time of his birth (indeed sometimes even before), for it is vital that his horoscope and that of his intended bride should be magically compatible."[27]

There are numerous systems of astrology. Of particular importance is the astrological birth chart for an individual, which is a picture of the positions of the sun, moon and planets at the precise moment of birth, relating (1) their precise positions in the Zodiac, and (2) the various aspects or angular relationships of these planets to each other. Charts depicting future influences, such as progressed and transiting charts can also be created from this birth chart combined with the appropriate projected chart. Charts present a complex interaction, relating various "planetary" qualities as they mix with the energies in the "sign of the Zodiac," and the harmony or disharmony of the aspects or angular relationships with other planets. All of this is synthesized when describing the individual. No simple art, it takes time to comprehend and utilize all this information properly. Again, like anything else, this science is occasionally misused.

Astrology is routinely dismissed by the scientific community, having an air of superstition about it, and because it cannot be explained in a causal way in terms of our present understanding of the physical universe. Most mainstream scientists find it difficult to believe that anyone could take astrology seriously. It is often suggested that only ancient or so-called "primitive" cultures that didn't know better, could believe such things. Typical arguments state that the ancients thought that celestial objects were only a short distance overhead, but modern man knows that the stars and the planets are enormously remote. However, this knowledge did not deter Sir Isaac Newton from finding value in astrology, or in the 20th Century Carl Jung, who found it to be a useful tool in working with his patients. Carl Jung attempted to explain phenomena such as astrology through a concept referred to as "synchronicity," an idea related to Swedenborg's Science of Correspondence, which will be discussed later.

However, mystics have known that the influence of the heavenly bodies upon us was in fact through the subtle bodies. The concept of subtle dark matter would therefore support this causal view, and provide a physical basis for astrology. Since the time-space of subtle matter is different from that of visible matter, then indeed, the dark matter energies directed at us from "distant" parts of our universe (say from the directions of constellations and heavenly bodies) which seem so distant in terms of our visible matter, may not be so distant in terms of the space-time of "dark subtle matter." These energies could, therefore, have a causal effect upon our subtle bodies, which in turn influences our entire being, subtle and gross. What we might see with our dark matter subtle body vision as we look out upon the universe would be very different from our ordinary vision. In the time-space of "dark matter," perhaps celestial objects <u>are</u> only a short distance overhead.

ANCIENT EGYPT

The wisdom of Ancient Egypt is expressed in writings by Emanuel Swedenborg, Rudolf Steiner, C.W. Leadbeater, Edouard Schure, and many others. They all tell us of a culture with advanced spiritual understandings, and a connection with the world of the deceased and beyond.

When it comes to other peoples beliefs, be it so called primitive cultures or ancient cultures, the Western world with its scientific perspective regards those views often as superstitious, and seldom suspects that there is anything of significance (particularly of scientific significance) that these cultures have to offer us. The tendency has been to disregard all mythic concepts as superstitious. We have "taught" other cultures to suppress their beliefs or understandings of the universe in our presence, and they obligingly do so. As a result, we miss out on some valuable concepts, knowledge, and wisdom. We always (and naturally so) try to analyze their lives in terms of our present understandings of the universe, i.e. in terms of what we presently "know," but to do so is to ignore the great potential for mystery, which may lead us far from our present limited understandings. Admittedly, this knowledge is difficult to explore since we in the Western world hardly know where to begin.

The Ancient Egyptians had a system of knowledge which accommodated the world we can see with our normal vision, but also included matter not visible to our ordinary vision. To them subtle dark matter was apparently as visible and as much a part of their world as visible matter, and they lived accordingly. They were aware of ten subtle bodies, 3 in the soul and spirit realm (Khu, Ba, Ka), 3 in the mental and emotional realm (Ab, Ren, and Schlem), 3 in the etheric realm (Sahu,

Khaibit, Khat) and one in the material realm (Aufu). Because of this understanding, they prepared well for their after death existence. This was paramount to their thinking, and how they lived, and how they died. A highly evolved culture, they knew that there were ways to affect the subtle matter through meaningful actions while still in the gross material realm, such as through spiritual ritual. The mummies of Egypt were symbols of transformation – preparation and assistance for the dying in the after death existence. They apparently had a better sense of the totality of their being than it seems we have today.

NEAR DEATH, AFTER DEATH AND REINCARNATION

"At the moment of death the empiric consciousness, or consciousness of objects, is lost. There is what is popularly called a 'swoon', which is, however, the corollary of super-consciousness itself, or the Clear Light of the Void; for the swoon is in, and of, the Consciousness as knower of objects (Vijnana Skandha). This empiric consciousness disappears, unveiling Pure Consciousness, which is ever ready to be 'discovered' by those who have the will to seek and the power to find it." W. Y. Evans-Wentz, The Tibetan Book of the Dead.

The knowledge of the subtle bodies makes an existence after death comprehensible. The subtle body doctrine provides a vehicle (the soul) for our existence after the death of our visible body. Obviously this existence would be very different from our life here in this dense physical world, but subtle bodies make the possibility real.

Near-Death and Out-of-Body Experiences

We cannot give adequate attention to this subject here, but there is extensive information given by Raymond Moody, Elizabeth Kubler Ross, and Stanislav Grof. But briefly, people having near-death experiences report experience of: leaving their visible body and observing themselves from a distance; having a form which varied from an amorphous cloud to energy patterns, or pure consciousness, or having a body, but one that was permeable, invisible, and inaudible to those in the phenomenal world; having feelings in some cases of confusion, in other cases ecstatic feelings of timelessness, weightlessness, serenity and tranquility; passing through a dark enclosed space such as a cave or tunnel; encountering other beings, such as dead relatives or friends, "guardian spirits," "spirit guides" or a "light being" who shows qualities of love, warmth, compassion and a sense of humor; communication through thought; a life review, self-judgment or divine judgment in which they describe an understanding of the consequences of their past actions and thoughts during their life. They frequently have knowledge of events which occurred at some distance from where their visible body was, and in many cases their knowledge of the event could be verified.

According to Barbara Harris, literature on the impact of near-death experiences on individuals shows that, "The first change that almost all experiencers have in common is that we are not afraid to die. The next change we talk about is how we feel about others. We care more, have greater compassion and feel love for everyone. At the same time our drive for material success decreases (to the dismay of close others) and *life becomes more precious.* It's as though we have taken a piece of the Light and brought it back with us and now we want and need to share it with others. And the more we give it away, the more we have to give."[28]

Near-death and out-of-body experiences, from the point of view of the subtle bodies and dark matter are the spontaneous awareness and identification with the subtle bodies, and the separation of these bodies from the visible body. It is not clear at

54

what level this separation occurs, which may vary depending upon the experience. Generally, for out-of-body experiences, the subtle bodies could separate at the level of the astral body, but for the near-death experiences, the separation would probably occur at the mental body or mano-maya-kosa, and/or the soul.

After Death

To most Westerners it may seem difficult to believe that any knowledge of after death could be obtained. However, mankind has traditionally taken after life existence for granted. If we have a physical soul composed of a very fine form of subtle dark matter, then it becomes easy to understand that some knowledge of after death could be acquired. The after death events appear to be very similar to near-death experiences. Discussions of the experiences which take place after death can be found in such books as *The Tibetan Book of the Dead, The Egyptian Book of the Dead,* Sogyal Rinpoche's book *The Tibetan Book of Living and Dying,* Rudolf Steiner's *Life Between Death and Rebirth,* and Kwasi Weridu's article *Death and the Afterlife in African Culture,* to name a few.

Although there appear to be differences in the specifics of the after death happenings, one must remember that the experiences of these states have a very different time-space relationship associated with them and far beyond our ability to comprehend from our present state of consciousness. Symbolic and representational art are therefore utilized to convey these after death events, as is some iconographical art of Tibetan Buddhism and shamanism. Although most Westerners would regard the after death experience a mystery about which one could only speculate, this is not true in many cultures. In most African cultures, for example, the deceased are still regarded as part of the community, and although they are rarely "seen," they nevertheless are participants. Kwasi Wiredu says that, "the traditional Ghanaian does not bifurcate the world into a natural and a supernatural world. Life after death is, for him, in a world closely continuous with the present one; and our departed ancestors are conceived still to be participating members of their families, rewarding good conduct and punishing its opposite in their own special way. The pouring of libation is, accordingly, intended as an invitation to them to come and take part in important undertakings of the living and to grant them their propitious auspices."[29] The deceased ancestors are highly valued. They are a bridge between the world of the living and the more refined spiritual world. Wiredu again states: "According to this conception, a human being has two types of constituents. The first is the material body as commonly perceived; this presents no immediate conceptual problems. The second, on the other hand, is not easy to characterize. ... The ontologically interesting thing about this kind of being is that although it is conceived in the *image* of a person, it is exempted from the grosser characteristics of the material body. Thus, it can appear at, or disappear from, places without regard to speed limits for matter in motion or to the laws of impenetrability. Moreover, it is capable of action at a distance in which a living person may be severely affected without perceptible contact. The question of perceivability brings us to an important property of the entities in question. They cannot be seen with the naked eye nor heard with the unaided ear, except on rare occasions when they themselves elect to make themselves sensibly accessible to particular persons; otherwise, they can be seen or heard only by people with medicinally heightened powers of sight and hearing."[30]

Reincarnation

Another common belief in mysticism and also numerous cultures throughout the world is reincarnation. In many third world cultures it is not unusual for individuals to recall a past life, and to know about the people who lived in the village of this previous existence. Only recently have children's recollections of past lives been researched and documented. There are several books which focus on children's past life memories, including *Children Who Remember Previous Lives: A Question of Reincarnation,* by Ian Stevenson, *Children's Past Lives*, by Carol Bowman, and *Old Souls: The Scientific Evidence for Past Lives,* by Tom Shroder. These books point to how relatively natural it is for children to recall past lives.

Dr. Ian Stevenson has scientifically investigated and documented hundreds of cases of reincarnation from all over the world. His approach was scrupulously scientific, meticulously gathering data and information from children's spontaneous past life memories, and exploring this information to verify the memories of the existence and events of these past lives.

Dr. Stevenson also discovered "that in 35 percent of his verified cases (309 of 895), the children had birthmarks or birth defects that matched wounds from their previous lives." These cases provide physical scientific evidence between the past and present life. "No matter how strong the verbal and behavioral evidence is in a case, critics will find fault with the data. But birth marks and birth defects – especially when they can be verified against medical records of the deceased – are undeniable, tangible evidence of a direct correspondence between a past and present life."[31]

An example is "an Indian boy who remembered being killed by a shotgun blast to his chest. On this boys chest was an array of birth marks that matched the pattern and location (verified by the autopsy report) of the fatal wounds."[32] The only reasonable explanation for Ian Stevenson's findings is reincarnation.

It is believed by mysticism, that upon death the causal body and the soul have a relatively longer existence. The more dense subtle bodies, the etheric and astral body, do not leave the visible body immediately upon death. With a dark matter subtle body that does not end at death (the soul), then reincarnation is clearly a possibility. It is generally believed that the kind of rebirth a person has is determined by the nature of one's actions in this life. However, "Those who master the laws of karma and achieve realization can choose to return in life after life to help others."[33] When one considers this issue deeply, it seems rather naïve to presume that our entire existence began with our birth on this planet, even though it is obvious that our visible bodies gave birth here.

SAVANT SYNDROME

Basically savants can be put into two categories: (1) An idiot savant is a person with autism that has extraordinary skills in certain domains in spite of cognitive deficiencies in most others, and (2) a prodigious savant, whose skill level would qualify him or her as a prodigy, or exceptional talent, even in the absence of a cognitive disability. These individuals have abilities that would be considered phenomenal or genius. Prodigious savants have traits such as seemingly limitless mnemonic skills, with many having eidetic or photographic memories.

The importance of the phenomena of the savant syndrome is our inability to explain it. No model of brain function will be complete until it can account for this condition. Almost all savants have a prodigious memory in common, a memory that appears to be exceedingly deep but very narrow – narrow in the sense that they have difficulty putting it to use.

Savant skills are usually found in one or more of 6 areas: calendar calculations, art, musical abilities, mathematics, spatial skills, and language skills.

Examples of idiot savants are (1) twin savants who could instantly name a day of the week over a 40,000 year span, and who may have an unlimited memory for numbers, and (2) Blind Tom who possessed a very low I.Q., but could play Mozart on the piano at age 4, and could play back flawlessly any piece of music, regardless of complexity. He could also repeat a discourse of any length in any language without the loss of a syllable.

Mathematical calculations performed mentally are relatively common in savants. Daniel Tammet (an autistic savant) says in his book *Born on a Blue Day*, "since early childhood, I have grown up with the ability to handle and calculate huge numbers in my head without any conscious effort. … In fact, this is a talent common to other real-life savants (sometimes referred to as 'lightning calculators'). … My favorite kind of calculation is power multiplication, which means multiplying a number by itself a specified number of times. … I see each result of a power multiplication as a distinctive visual pattern in my head. As the sums and their results grow, so the mental shapes and colors I experience become increasingly more complex. I see 37's fifth power – $37 \times 37 \times 37 \times 37 \times 37 = 69,343,957$ as a large circle composed of smaller circles running clockwise from the top around. … I never wrote anything down when I calculated because I could always do the multiplication in my head. … When multiplying, I see the two numbers as distinct shapes. The image changes and a third shape emerges – the correct answer."[34]

As mentioned, the savant syndrome is impossible to explain with our present day understanding of science and the brain. But it appears to us that individuals with savant syndrome are connecting directly with something deeper. Perhaps when the brain developed, something was left "open," allowing these individuals to connect more directly with subtle bodies, but unfortunately creating other physical problems. We feel the imagery described by Daniel Tammet is an experience on some level of the deeper subtle body processes at work.

In what we feel to be a related issue, there is the story of Ernest Newman, (a well known English music critic and author of numerous books on music and composers), who said he would read musical scores for pleasure. By looking at the scores he could hear the music in his head, but the music he heard was better than the actual performance because there were no playing errors, and the music had PERFECT PURE TONES. Again, such purity does not exist in this world, but it does in the world of subtle bodies, or in Plato's forms (see chapter 3). One could easily imagine that great composers, such as Mozart and Beethoven, may well have had this ability.

CONSCIOUSNESS

"One thing can be claimed in favour of the mystical teaching of the 'identity' of all minds with each other and with the supreme mind – as against the fearful monadology of Leibniz. The doctrine of identity can claim that it is clinched by the empirical fact that consciousness is never experienced in the plural, only in the singular. Not only has none of us experienced more than one consciousness, but there is also no trace of circumstantial evidence of this ever happening anywhere in the world. If I say that there cannot be more than one consciousness in the same mind, this seems to blunt tautology – we are quite unable to imagine the contrary." – Erwin Schrödinger, Mind and Matter

Questions such as "what is consciousness?" or "what is the physical basis of consciousness?" have not been successfully even approached by Western science. This is an area that science cannot touch. The prevailing view of Western scientists is that the brain creates consciousness. Steven Hawking says, "I regard the brain as a computer which will stop working when its components fail. There is no heaven or afterlife for broken-down computers. That is a fairy story for people afraid of the dark." While it is true that the brain stops working at death, it does not necessarily follow that consciousness ceases to exist. Mystical teachings would suggest that the basis of consciousness is deeper than the physical brain. Those who study the brain professionally in the west have often avoided the question entirely. In psychology, cognitive psychologists have been able to explore learning, memory, and perception; and neuroscientists have been able to explore the neurological system, but none of this tells us why we experience our existence at all. As in all of Western science, serious theories of consciousness have been hard to come by. Recent popular books on consciousness by Francis Crick, Daniel Dennett, and Roger Penrose, and academic journals devoted to the subject, have stimulated discussion.

We should distinguish between the issue of connecting neural mechanism with cognitive functions (such as the ability to discriminate and categorize stimuli, the capacity to verbalize mental states, the distinction between waking and sleeping states of mind); and the heart of the consciousness issue, why is there awareness at all – why are we not unaware mechanical robots? Even Crick and Penrose concede that so far they have not made any inroads into this issue. When it comes to the basic problem of conscious awareness, all the quantum mechanics and parapsychology in the world does not add up to a solution.

To fully understand the nature of consciousness, one must understand the subtle bodies. There is a unique time-space associated with each type of subtle matter making up our subtle bodies. To experience the various levels of human consciousness, one must be able to experience the various subtle bodies. We tend to make the mistake of believing when we observe an object, such as a rock, that we as conscious beings are observing a non-conscious object. However, consciousness cannot take place in a vacuum. Consciousness requires both the observer and the observed object; it is an interplay between the two. So both you and the rock are a part of the phenomena of consciousness. Just as mass, charge, time, and space are basic components of the universe, and cannot be explained in terms of anything more basic, so consciousness is a basic property of the universe and cannot be explained in terms of anything more basic. Since the quality of consciousness experienced correlates with the type of time-space-matter one is experiencing, ultimately, the space-time-matter interplay must equate to consciousness. Time and space being dependent upon the form of matter one is dealing with or is conscious of. It would appear then that consciousness on the subjective level equates to matter and the time-space associated with it on the objective level. One cannot say which causes which, or which is more fundamental, and, therefore, ultimately, consciousness and matter are the same thing. When one experiences pure consciousness, there is no distinction between observed and observer. Consciousness is something as basic as the universe itself.

MORPHOGENESIS

The complex transformation of a seed to a plant or a fertilized egg to an animal is incredible to behold, and cannot be simply attributed to some sort of genetically engineered and highly organized chemical reactions. Something much more seems to be going on here. Despite all our remarkable advances in genetics and our ability to manipulate genes, we still do not understand the morphogenesis of a living system.

To account for this "miracle," the seventeenth century offered "preformation," the idea that the seed or egg contained a microscopic version of the adult organism. Scientists went so far as to claim that they saw, and made drawings of, these minute human figures (homunculi) under the microscope. More recent recommendations suggested that morphogenesis was organized by fields. However what these fields are, and the mechanism by which these fields operate remains a mystery. Rupert Sheldrake says: "What exactly are morphogenetic fields? How do they work? Despite the widespread use of this concept within biology, there are no clear answers to these questions. Indeed, the nature of these fields has remained as mysterious as morphogenesis itself."[35] Rupert Sheldrake has gone on to state that morphogenetic fields are physically real and that a transfer of information can occur through "morphic resonance," so that every living thing contributes its experience to a collective "memory pool." For example, the knowledge that rats obtain through training in New England in order to escape a tank, can be "picked up" by not only the next generation of rats, but rats in Australia as well. By adding this property of resonance to morphic fields, the existence of morphic fields has become more testable, and the experimental evidence increases.

However, the concept of morphogenic fields presently has no defined physical basis. The method by which it would operate is unknown, and as a result more precise experimentation is limited. One cannot explain why morphic resonance enhances the learning ability of mice, but fails to enhance the mathematical ability of our high school students. One cannot say how to go about eliminating the phenomena or enhancing it. As a physical basis, Sheldrake has eliminated electromagnetic energy as a carrier of morphic resonance. By doing so, one would have to conclude that the physical basis to morphic resonance is a presently unknown form of energy produced by a presently unknown source of matter. Our understanding of subtle bodies would suggest then that morphogenetic fields are in actuality a part of the dark matter subtle body theory. It is the subtle bodies which control morphogenesis, and it is the subtle bodies which allow "morphic resonance" to occur.

GEOGENESIS AND THE GAIA HYPOTHESIS

The existence of an earth spirit has been with us since most ancient times. John Michell says, "The earth was sacred, not because pious people chose so to regard it, but because it was in fact ruled by spirit, by the creative powers of the universe, manifest in all phenomena of nature, shaping the features of the landscape, regulating the seasons, the cycles of fertility, the lives of animals and men."[36] In a similar vein, the alchemist Basilius Valentinus said that, "The earth is not a dead body, but is inhabited by a spirit that is its life and soul. All created things, minerals included, draw their strength from the earth spirit. This spirit is life, it is nourished in the stars, and it gives nourishment to all living beings it shelters in its womb."[37] The Chinese system of Feng-shui, which has gained popularity in the west as of late, is also based on the earth spirit.

Very recently the concept of "Gaia" has entered the thinking of the scientific community. The Gaia hypothesis (named after the Greek Earth Spirit Goddess) was put forth by James Lovelock to account for how the earth and its environment is able to support life. He proposes that the earth behaves as if it were a living, conscious organism. It appears to him that "the self-regulation of climate and chemical composition is a process that emerges from the tightly coupled evolution of rocks, air, and ocean – in addition to that of organisms. Such interlocking self-regulation, while rarely optimal – consider the cold and hot places of the Earth, the wet and the dry – nevertheless keeps the earth a fit place for life."[38] Scientific evidence for this hypothesis continues to mount.

Perhaps it should not be surprising, then, that the mystics regard the earth itself as having subtle bodies. The earth is apparently immersed in dark matter subtle bodies, some of which extend beyond the atmosphere. Living on this planet, perhaps we live in the earth's dark matter subtle bodies. "Like the energies of the human body, the spirit of the earth flows through the surface in channels or veins, and between the two energy currents of man and earth there exists a natural affinity that enables men to divine the presence and local character of the earth spirit, to intuit how best to bring human ways into harmony with it, and even, by the exercise of will and imagination to influence its flow."[39] Consistent with this is the view of Pierre Teilhard de Chardin who sees that "from the biosphere (the layer of living things covering the earth) has emerged the noosphere (a mind layer surrounding the earth). This mind layer, or human consciousness, generates increasingly complex social arrangements that in turn give rise to a higher consciousness. Ultimately, the evolutionary process culminates in the convergence of the material and the spiritual into a superconsciousness that Teilhard called the Omega Point. By his love, this God-Omega attracts and thereby gives direction to the whole evolutionary process."[40]

COSMOGENESIS
(Also See Chapter III, A New Cosmology)

The prevailing scientific view of the universe suggests that the laws governing the universe were created in the first few minutes (if not seconds) after the big bang, and that from then on the universe proceeded as if it were a blind, indifferent machine, simply obeying its laws of physics. This indifferent mechanical machine could, for all science knows, go on just as it does without there being grief or joy, emotion, effort, responsibility or consciousness connected with it, which there obviously is.

This may well be how the universe appears from the point of view of luminous or "charged" matter. However, if we take subtle matter into account, we may discover a living, breathing, learning universe that is user friendly. Consider the mystical view of the universe. Consider where subtle dark matter came from. Our scientific understanding of the big bang as a single energy event which presumably created simultaneously all matter and time and space, is, interestingly enough, not the likely source of the dark matter we are discussing. The traditional view of mysticism is that the more dense forms of matter were born out of the finer forms of matter, a Creation which is divided into seven major planes of consciousness or matter. Our present scientific understanding of the origins of the Universe indicates that all matter was created out of the big bang about 13.82 billion years ago. Our knowledge of this event is sufficient to suggest that subtle "dark matters" may not have been formed in that event, but existed before the big bang, at least before the final "explosion" which produced charged matter.

The experimental evidence for the big bang is based on the behavior of visible (luminous) matter. Although there are many ideas associated with the expanding and cooling of the universe, the firmly established supporting evidence for the big bang theory is: (1) the red shift observed of light coming from distant galaxies, which first suggested that the universe was expanding, (2) the microwave background radiation of the universe (the "echo" of the big bang), which is a sea of thermal radiation, (3) primordial nucleosynthesis (big bang atomic nuclear production), related to the amount of deuterium, helium, and lithium created at the big bang, and (4) the observation made of extremely distant galaxies which shows distinct evidence that they are younger than nearby older galaxies. These observations are based on radiation producing (luminous or charged matter). We can no longer assume that all forms of matter, i.e., both luminous and "dark," were created at the big bang, even though luminous matter clearly was. The big bang could have occurred in an ocean of subtle dark matter. While this may seem like a highly speculative consideration, it is equally speculative to presume that all forms of matter, including "dark matter," were created out of the big bang. Thus the concept of dark matter necessitates the need to reconsider the presently held belief that nothing existed (except perhaps a singularity) prior to the big bang. Mysticism might say that we are composed of sheaths of matter, matter which was created at each major event in the universe, when this series of events led to the "condensation" or formation of various types of matter, from pure spirit (the most subtle form of matter) to the last of these "events," the big bang, which was the beginning of our visible matter.

A great mystery in the creation of the universe, which still exists in the scientific community, is the nature of physical laws which allowed for life to have formed in the universe. Scientists have discovered that if the laws of physics are changed ever so slightly, nothing resembling life could have formed. Science has no explanation for this cosmological coincidence, how just the right physical laws could have been produced, since science doesn't believe consciousness was present (or anything else except perhaps a singularity) at the big bang. Scientists believe consciousness came only as life formed.

The existence of subtle dark matter at the time of the big bang may explain the cosmological issue concerning why matter is not spread evenly throughout the universe, as cosmologists would expect. Instead the stars are gathered into galaxies, galaxies are gathered into groups and clusters, and these, in turn, are gathered into superclusters. Until about 300,000 years after the big bang, the visible matter in the Universe was a hot, turbulent plasma. "If any clumping had started, the intense pressure of the radiation in the plasma would have blown it apart. Only after 300,000 years or so, when the Universe had cooled off to the point that those nuclei could capture electrons (and thus become the atoms we are familiar with) could gravitational collecting get started. Unfortunately for Cosmologists, by then it was too late – not only was matter too thinly spread to form superclusters, clusters and groups, it was too diffuse even to make the kinds of galaxies we see all around us."[41] What is needed to account for this is dark matter which is unaffected by this intense electromagnetic radiation, i.e. matter not composed of charged particles, an example of which is subtle dark matter. Intense radiation would pass through this dark matter and it would not experience the intense pressure. Thus the formation of clumps early on would be possible. Measurements made by the Cosmic Background Explorer satellite (COBE) of radiation emitted around this time of interest shows that visible matter in the universe was indeed highly clustered. Physicists have hypothesized a class of dark matter subatomic particles known as weakly interacting massive particles (WIMPs) which could explain the clustering. WIMPs would have been produced at the big bang, are without charge, but would be more massive than the neutrons and protons which make up the nucleus of the atom. Some evidence suggests that WIMPs do exist, but even if they are discovered can they possibly account for all the dark matter in the universe? Remember, dark matter is no minor player in the universe, accounting for 26.8% of the mass/energy of the universe, which is over 50 times all the billions of stars in all the billions of galaxies. WIMPs are a possible candidate for some of the dark matter, but subtle dark matter suggested by mystical teachings seems like a much more likely candidate.

From the point of view of subtle matter, it would appear that the big bang could be correlated with the Creation of the Universe, as well as the decent of man, since it is associated with the creation of our dense matter from pure spirit (and thus the consciousness associated with our dense matter). So we can see this event as the descent of man, the fall of man and the universe from pure spirit to dense matter. James Joyce's image for the fall of man in *Finnegans Wake* is presented as follows:

"The fall (bababadalgharaghtakamminarronnkonnbronn-tonnerronntuonnthunntrovarrhounawnskawntoohoohoor-denenthurnuk!) of a once wallstrait oldparr is retaled early in bed and later on life down through all Christian minstrelsy."[42]

The word in parentheses representing the fall of man is made up of syllables from words utilized for thunder from various cultures. This word depicts the father of all thunders, which is a good poetic description of the big bang, and also the decent of man and the universe from pure spirit to dense matter.

Combining the fall of man with the Creation of this universe reminds one of William Blake's view of creation. He believes this "familiar world was created only after a cosmic catastrophe. When the life of the spirit was reduced to a sea of atoms, the Creator set a limit below which it could not deteriorate farther, and began creating the world of nature. The longer books that Blake wrote describe Los's creation of animals and people within the world of nature. ... In believing that creation followed a cosmic catastrophe and a fall of spiritual beings into matter, Blake recalls Gnosticism, a multi-faceted religious movement which has run parallel to mainstream Christianity. Unlike most other Gnosticizers, Blake considered our own world to be a fine and wonderful place, but one which would ultimately give way to a restored universe."[43]

"PLANES" OF SUBTLE MATTER

The concept of "planes" of subtle matter as described by mystics could be interpreted by physics today as "atoms" which are composed of different, non-electrical forces. Just as visible atoms interact through electric charge, other "planes" of matter interact through other forces, such as qi-force or mano-force, etc. Western science cannot say exactly what matter is, or why it was created; science can only determine the forces and principles governing its behavior within defined situations. Physicists today feel that they have an excellent grasp of the physical laws governing atomic matter through quantum mechanics. But these laws govern visible matter and may only be a special case of more generalized principles governing other subtle forms of atomic matter. Who is to say that there is only one type of atomic matter composed of atoms which are held together by the electrical force? Mysticism tells us otherwise, and modern physics cannot disprove this physical basis of mysticism. Clearly subtle matter is quite different from visible matter, not only having different binding forces, but also not having a nucleus composed of heavy nucleons like our familiar atomic matter. It is apparently self-luminous, yet a mountain of uncharged "atomic" matter could pass right through the very room one is sitting in, and one would not know it. One could not see, touch, hear, taste or smell it.

This idea of other types of atomic matter would suggest the possibility of a 3-dimensional periodic table, as shown in Figure 3. Using the subtle body/subtle matter system of India, just as electric charge interacts strongly with electric charge, prana-matter would interact strongly with prana-matter, and mano-matter would interact strongly with mano-matter, etc. However, there must also be a weaker interaction between charged matter and prana matter, and between prana and mano matter, etc., or there would be no communication or interaction between these different levels ("planes") of matter. Apparently charged matter would not interact directly with mano matter, etc., according to the accounts of some mystics, but would have to interact through the intermediate types of matter. We must keep in mind that prana matter, mano matter, etc., are extraordinary types of matter, not like the relatively "dead" electrically charged matter of our normal experience. Our Western science has certainly made remarkable discoveries by focusing on this "visible" matter, and one can easily say that never has humankind understood charged "visible" matter so thoroughly. But one can also say that never before has mankind been so ignorant of these other subtle forms of matter.

Figure 3. The 3-Dimensional Periodic Table

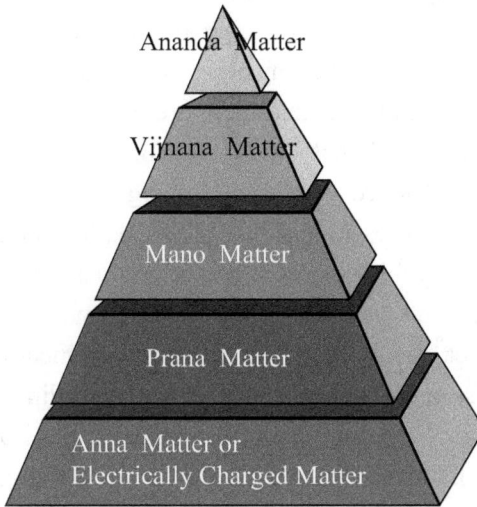

CONCLUSION

The ideas suggested in this book provide a very significant and powerful paradigm shift which will impact all of our Western sciences and the way we relate to the universe. This does not negate what science has discovered to date, but will certainly require the application of more generalized scientific principles. For, when you weigh all the evidence, the inescapable conclusion is that the mystics were right about the physical nature of the universe, that there are multiple "planes" matter, or types of atoms. What better way to account for the growing scientific evidence for subtle energies (qi, prana, ki, etc.), paranormal senses (clairvoyance, telepathy, telekinetics, remote viewing), psychic healing (hands on healing, healing through prayer), morphogenesis, geogenesis, cosmogenesis, out-of-body experiences, near-death experiences, reincarnation, spiritual encounters, and other related phenomena outlined in this book?

In reviewing Western scientific development, we see that one hundred years ago atoms were thought to be solid, indivisible particles and therefore could not interpenetrate with other atoms. Mysticism still maintained that the subtle interpenetrating bodies made of "matter from other planes" did exist. With the development of quantum mechanics, the atom took on a different picture, having a very heavy but extremely small nucleus surrounded by very low mass electrons. The atom did have a solid appearance from the point of view of the electric field, but from the point of view of mass is was quite empty. Uncharged particles could easily penetrate and pass through the atom. Since electromagnetism was found to be also responsible for vision as well as atomic properties, "atoms" held together by some force other than the electromagnetic force would be invisible to our normal vision and could interpenetrate with visible atoms. These "subtle atoms" could interact with each other through their own respective binding force, much like visible atoms interact with each other through their binding electromagnetic force. In some ways it is surprising that modern scientists have never suggested such an idea.

This possibility makes the knowledge which mystics have obtained about other types of matter, subtle matter, or planes of matter in the universe, a reality. Their understanding that we are made up of subtle bodies made from these other types of matter, is compelling. If humankind was indeed composed of subtle bodies made up of different types of subtle "dark matter," and if we were capable of becoming conscious of these subtle bodies, then we would indeed experience the world of that type of matter, much like mysticism states. Just as our dense bodies primarily interact through electromagnetic energy, (the energy holding atoms together), so it is possible that subtle matter interacts through the energy which holds subtle matter "atoms" together. And this energy, call it qi or prana, would not readily interact with our visible matter.

This type of subtle matter would fall into Western science's broad category of "dark matter," because it would not be visible to our ordinary vision, but having mass could produce gravitational effects. We could be immersed in subtle matter and would not know it. Therefore, it seems that we can begin to accept the physical description of the universe that mysticism provides.

As evidence for the existence of such subtle "dark matter," we need only look at the growing scientific evidence for phenomena such as qi or prana, psychic healing, the power of prayer, paranormal phenomena (clairvoyance, telepathy, telekinetics, remote viewing, divining), morphogenesis, transpersonal experiences, out-of-body experiences, near-death experiences, reincarnation, etc. These phenomena cannot be explained in terms of our present understanding of the forces in the universe, but are easily understood in terms of our subtle bodies and subtle matter.

When we look at the recent scientific developments of dark matter we discover that dark matter forms a network throughout the universe, interconnecting the galaxies.

The subtle body doctrine of mysticism has passed the test of time, being a part of our most ancient to modern cultures, throughout the world. It provides an excellent foundation for the explanation of numerous phenomena so that even without a physical basis it is a valuable system well worth exploring and utilizing. Its success in mystical traditions and the scientific verification of much of the phenomena mentioned here are sufficient to warrant subtle body theory as a valuable doctrine. Truly, it needs no further proof. However, the recent scientific concept of dark matter provides a new understanding of what the mystics refer to as subtle matter, and so the possibility for a connection between mysticism and Western science is quite real and could be of great benefit.

This suggests that we have a soul, and it is physical, even though it is a very fine form of physical dark matter. But we must be aware that intellectual understanding of this doctrine will not enlighten mankind; we must obtain an experiential awareness of the subtle bodies in order to truly benefit from these teachings. In so doing, we will be able to live our lives from a deeper understanding of the nature of man and of our position in the universe. We will better understand the repercussions of our actions and decisions, on a personal level, a social level, and a global level. The importance of this transition for humankind cannot be overestimated.

From the point of view of physics, dark matter is just as real as visible matter, even though it is a subtler form of matter. With "dark matter," science will have many new frontiers to explore, unimaginable to the scientists of today. The impact that dark matter will have on science in the 21st Century may be greater than the impact of knowledge gained from quantum mechanics in the 20th Century. Science will be exploring a subtle matter and a subtle human anatomy and physiology. Although there have been significant explorations of subtle energies, further explorations of the subtle energies may be more successful and expansive in view of this new understanding. We can better approach this problem perhaps by using meditative techniques to aid us in our awareness of the subtle bodies, and to observe the world objectively from that perspective. This may aid Western scientists to better understand the interactions which dark matter has, particularly with visible matter. Mainstream scientists are not presently looking for dark matter in man. They should. The details of how the subtle bodies and chakras interact with the world around them and with the visible body need to be better understood, although we have a great legacy of mysticism to aid us. I suspect that we will not be able to apply Western scientific methodology effectively until we can experience subtle matter directly. Science will then undergo a significant revolution in its thinking and its methodology.

Intellectually understanding the subtle bodies is not sufficient to experience them. And to grow spiritually we must experience the subtle bodies and their respective realms. As Ken Wilber states:

> "Perhaps you can start to see why even the great wisdom traditions (with their epistemological pluralism) can offer such a devastating critique of the notion that a 'new paradigm' in science would, or even could, be equivalent to a spiritual opening. For what is required is not a new monological science or a new dialogical interpretation, but a genuine method for directly opening

to translogical contemplation, and no new scientific paradigm whatsoever has been able to make that offer."[44]

Also, he states:

"Has there been a recent revolution in science, a genuine new paradigm in science itself that is holistic rather than atomistic? Yes, definitely. There have been several of them, actually, including various aspects of quantum physics, relativistic physics, cybernetics, dynamical systems theory, autopoieses, chaos theory, and complexity theory. These are all new revolutions, new paradigms in the true sense, with new modes of research, new social practices supporting them, new types of data, new forms of evidence, and new theories surrounding them.

"But they are all, without exception, monological to the core. And thus, as important as they are in their own right, they have little to offer us in terms of actually integrating monological with dialogical and translogical – that is, integrating science and spirituality."[45]

Today scientists are looking for dark matter in distant galaxies, never considering that mankind may be composed of the very substance they seek to understand. Scientists regard dark matter as one little piece in their puzzle, never suspecting that this piece is the beginning of a greater puzzle. We need only to look within ourselves, both physically and spiritually to make this discovery. To understand how science can bridge this gap, we must look into the "science" commonly used by the mystics to elicit, to experience these greater truths. We will see in the remaining chapters how our view of science must be expanded in order for these experiences to occur.

CHAPTER 3

A NEW COSMOLOGY

PRELIMINARY REMARKS

Our universe "exploded" into existence about 13.82 billion years ago, according to the results of the Planck space telescope. At present we can say that the mass/energy of the universe is made up of about 68.3% dark energy; 26.8% dark matter; and only about 5% "normal matter" (stars, heavy elements, neutrinos, and free hydrogen and helium). This 5% also represents what we know about the universe. The other 95% (dark matter and dark energy) is still a complete mystery in to the scientific community.

BEFORE THE BEGINNING: THE PRE-UNIVERSE

Physicists and Cosmologists frequently state that the universe was created "out of nothing," but that is not quite what they mean. What they mean is that the universe was created out of nothing physical. If we look at the beginning of our Universe (what physicists call the Big Bang), we discover that out of this initiating event came **mass, time and space.** If physicists and cosmologists are correct, then we can readily conclude that before the Big Bang there was **no mass, no time, and no space**. So whatever existed before the Big Bang was **non- physical**, and existed outside of time, and had no space as we know it. That is actually a lot to know, as we shall see. Needless to say, this "pre-universe" condition is outside of our worldly human experience. Within this "pre-universe realm" we would have to throw out anything and everything that we can conceive of or imagine, because all of our knowledge is based in our physical reality.

Still, we can conclude the following about the pre-universe condition.

1. As already stated, the pre-universe condition was not physical – it had no mass. That is **not** to say that this is "nothing." It **IS** nothing physical, but that does not mean it's nothing. Even within our universe, there are non-physical things. You may want to consider that – we will come back to this point later.

2. The pre-universe has no "time," since "time" was created at the Big Bang. What does it mean to have no time? For one, this would mean that whatever the universe "erupted" out of, had/has no ability to change – it is unchangeable/fixed. Change is a sign of time, as is motion. To not have "time" means that no change can occur, and no motion occurs. That should not be a problem, since there is nothing physical to change or move, and no "space" to move in. So another way of stating this is that you cannot add anything to or take anything away from the pre-universe, because that would be a change, and change can occur only in time.

Equally fascinating is the logical conclusion that being outside of time means that the pre-universe must always "exist," non-physically of course. So, whatever existed before the Big Bang must still be with us today, as well as yesterday and tomorrow - it must be eternal. So, it's right here with us in the universe, always. The pre-universe did not **change** into a universe (that, again, would indicate time), but stayed with its creation.

3. Another "property" we can give to the non-physical pre-universe is that it has **enormous potential**. We say this because it obviously had the potential to create an entire universe – to create everything in it, everything that is, has been, or ever will be in the universe. We know this to be true because it has been **actualized (or will be actualized)**. And we are not talking about only nouns, but verbs as well, since action or motion could not exist in the pre-universe. So think of all the galaxies, stars, planets, plants, animals, rocks, etc., (as well as all the various forms of consciousness associated with living organisms), that ever have existed or ever will exist on all the countless billions of planets throughout the universe, and all the actions they are capable of, and we can say without a doubt that the non-physical pre-universe had/has the potential to create at least this much. That is **ENORMOUS potential**. And we cannot say that this non-physical pre-universe has the potential of creating only one universe - in fact it may be capable of creating countless universes, with complex systems unknown to this universe. In fact physicists today speculate about multiverses (many universes), and we cannot presently put a limit on what kinds of universes are possible. So to say that the pre-universe had/has "**ENORMOUS potential**" seems to be truly an understatement.

What is fascinating to us is that numerous cultures have similar concepts with essentially the same properties. For example in Buddhism – the dharmakaya; in the Kabbalah – Ein Sof; in Taoism – the Tao, or the Tao which can't be spoken; in Hinduism – the Akashic Field; in ancient Greece/Rome – the Elysian Fields; in Christianity – God the Father; in Platonism – Plato's Forms; and in Physics – the Vacuum Energy, to name a few. All of these concepts suggest something which cannot truly be named because we use names for physical objects, and so to name the pre-universe is misleading – still it seems we need a term to refer to it by, so we can talk about it. But how could these other cultures arrive at this idea before scientists even discovered the Big Bang (an idea that is less than 100 years old)?

Since a complete examination of these ideas is way beyond the scope of this book, we will very briefly look at a few of these concepts listed here, to see if we may be able to refine our understanding of the non-physical pre-universe.

Physics and the Vacuum Energy (Absolute Space)

At this point, we need to distinguish between relative space and absolute space. By absolute space, we will mean the vacuum, or the inherent properties of the vacuum, the vacuum energy. By relative space, we will mean the space created by matter. Relative space is measured relative to matter, and it has the dimensionality of the matter we are discussing. Relative space has to do with lengths and areas and volumes, but not with the inherent properties of the space. Absolute space is independent of the type of matter we are discussing; it exist where there is space and where there is matter.

The vacuum energy of the universe is considered by physicists to be filled with "virtual particles," particles which have the potential to manifest physically out of the vacuum. We cannot talk about the distance between virtual particles, or the number of virtual particles in a given space, or any properties of virtual particles which we typically associate with the physical universe; that is until the virtual particles manifest physically.

Here "space" is being used in the absolute sense:
"The view that space is empty and passive, and not even real to boot, is in complete opposition to the view we get from contemporary physics Even if physicists typically refuse to speculate on the ultimate nature of reality ... it is clear that what

they describe as the unified vacuum – the seat of all the fields and forces of the physical world – is in fact the primary reality of the universe Out of it sprung the particles that make up our universe, and when the last of the supergalactic black holes "evaporates," it is into it that the particles fall back again. What we think of as matter is but the quantised semi-stable bundling of the energies that spring from the vacuum. In the last count matter is but a waveform disturbance in the nearly infinite energy-sea that is the fundamental medium – and hence the primary reality – of this universe, and of all universes that ever existed and will ever exist. [46]

It would seem that every point in the vacuum is indistinguishable, and contains all the laws of physics, which all determines the behavior of all matter.

The Dharmakaya: Dharma - Truth, kaya – form or body.

In Buddhism, the dharmakaya can be defined as the embodiment of all the known, all laws, all forms or experiences, all existence. It is part of the Trikaya Doctrine, which also includes the Sambogakaya and the Nirmanakaya.

There are 3 terms commonly used to express the dharmakaya. They are: "Unborn," "Unceasing," "Unoriginated." If you look at this brief description of the dharmakaya, we see that it matches quite well with the non-physical pre-universe. The terms "Unborn," "Unceasing," and "Unoriginated" are properties associated with existing outside of time, as mentioned earlier. And "the embodiment of all known, all laws, all forms of experience, all existence," are the properties associated with the enormous potential of our non-physical pre-universe.

Ein-Sof

Ein Sof may be translated as "no end," "unending," "there is no end," or "infinite."

According to the Kabbalah, BEFORE ANYTHING emanated, there was only Ein Sof. Ein Sof was all that existed. Similarly, after it brought into being that which exists (our physical universe), there is nothing but it. You cannot find anything that exists apart from it. The boundless is called Ein Sof, Infinite. It is absolute undifferentiation in perfect, changeless oneness. Since it is boundless, there is nothing outside of it. Since it transcends and conceals itself, it is the essence of everything hidden and revealed. Again, being outside of time it stays with us throughout time.

Taoism – The Tao

Tao literally means "the path" or "The Way." The Tao is the unproduced producer of all that is, a harmonious power that flows throughout the universe.

In his explanation of the universe Lao-tzu wrote:

There is a thing confusedly formed,
Born before heaven and earth,
Silent and void
It stands alone and does not change
Goes round and does not weary,
It is capable of being the mother of the world.
I know not its name
So I style it "the way."

The Akashic Field

The overall idea behind the concept of an Akashic Field is that behind the materialistic and mechanistic world there is in fact another realm of interaction. Ervin Laszlo says about the Akashic Field that *"the universe we observe and inhabit is a secondary product of the energy sea that was there before there was anything there at all. Hindu and Chinese cosmologies have always maintained that the things and beings that exist in the world are a concretization or distillation of the basic energy of the cosmos, descending from its original source. The physical world is a reflection of energy vibrations from more subtle energy fields. Creation and all subsequent existence, is a progression downward and outward from the primordial source.*

In Indian philosophy the ultimate end of the physical world is a return to Akasha, its original subtle-energy womb. At the end of time as we know it, the almost infinitely varied things and forms of the manifest world dissolve into formlessness, living beings exist in a state of pure potentiality, and dynamic functions condense into static stillness. In Akasha, all attributes of the manifest world merge into a state that is beyond attributes: the state of Brahman."[47]

Plato's Forms

The idea of Plato's "Forms" is central to his philosophy. In Plato's "Forms" we find a particularly interesting perspective on the universe. Plato saw the universe as having 3 kinds of things in it: (1) physical objects, (2) "mental" objects including thoughts and emotions, and (3) abstract things having no spacial or temporal properties, which are referred to as "Forms" or

"Ideas." Nobody argues with the existence of physical things and mental things, but the concept of "abstract" things is a little harder to grasp. Physical objects are what we normally think our physical universe as being composed of. "Mental" things we do not normally think of as physical, although in the previous chapter, we suggested that "mental" things are properties of "subtle" matter. Anyway, "mental" things are "time" related – thoughts come and go, as do emotions. Being "time" related they are part of the universe and not the pre-universe. Now it is tempting to put "abstract" things in the category of "mental." However they are different from mental objects like "thoughts" and "emotions" in that, when properly understood, they are NOT "time" related - they are permanent and unchanging.

Plato argued logically about the unique existence of these Forms. He asserts that Forms, and not the material world of change known to us through sensation, possess the highest and most fundamental kind of reality. Only knowledge of the Forms constitutes real knowledge.

According to Plato, a Form is an abstract property or quality. If you consider any property of an object you can separate it from that object and consider the property by itself; you are then contemplating a Form. For example, if you separate the roundness of a baseball or tennis ball from its color, its weight, texture, and consider just the quality of roundness, then you are thinking of the Form of roundness. We can also consider the Form of Beauty, or the Form of musical notes, or even the Form of running. Plato held that this property existed apart from the object. The abstract property (Form) exists in a realm **separate** from the object; the Form exists independently of the object and independently of thought. For example, all round objects copy this same Form of roundness.

Plato points out that the Forms themselves are transcendent; they do not exist in space and time. A material object, such as a baseball, exists at a particular time and space. The Form of roundness, exists in a different way, because a Form such as roundness will never change; it does not exist in time. Roundness is the same at all times or places (space) in which it might be instantiated, and it can be instantiated in many places at once. However, it need not be instantiated at all in order for the Form to exist. The Form of roundness can be found in many particular spatial locations, and even if all round objects were destroyed, the property of roundness would still exist.

It is important to note that Forms are also "pure" or "ideal." In our physical world, a perfect sphere or a perfect circle does not exist, yet we use the concept of the perfect sphere or circle to identify round objects. In other words we use this pure property when we relate to the physical object. A material object, such as a baseball, has many properties: shape, texture, color, hardness, etc. These properties are all put together to make up this individual baseball. As pointed out, a Form is just one of these properties, existing by itself apart from space and time. Roundness is just pure roundness, without any other properties mixed in. The Forms differ from material objects, then, in that they are transcendent and pure, while material objects are complex conglomerations of properties located in space and time.

One should also notice that all disciplines utilize ideal Forms. The sciences, all the liberal arts, all of our curriculum, are base on ideal Forms. For example in mathematics, we have ideal concepts such as straight lines, parallel lines, circles, spheres, etc., all ideal concepts and none of which exist as pure in the physical world. Where do they exist? In Physics we have Newton's Laws, and Maxwell's Equations, and Schrödinger's Equation, etc. These equations are ideal equations which do not exist in the physical world we study – we cannot say that F=ma is exactly true. It is only as true to the extent which we can measure it – even if that's 20 places of accuracy, will it be correct to 30 places, what about 100 places? In music we have ideal notes in our musical scale, but no such pure note exists in the physical world. In Law we have concepts of Justice and Truth, which again are ideals. Everything we learn, when we look at it carefully, is communicated through ideal concepts or Forms.

So, this pureness of Forms can be viewed as the ideal models for all of the properties that are present in physical objects. The Forms are the perfect examples of the properties they instantiate, even though the perfect example does not exist in the physical world. The material world is only similar to the more real world of Forms. The Form of roundness, for example, is the perfect model of roundness. So the Forms are ultimately real. Material objects are, in a sense, images or copies of these perfectly real Form objects. Material objects could not possibly be pure; they could at best be **"copies"** or **"images"** (as Plato calls them) of underlying realities which can be thought about but which **cannot be perceived.**

Now, the Forms are the actual causes of all that exists in this world. The Forms make it possible for us to recognize objects, to talk about or describe objects, and are thus the source of the intelligibility of all material objects. The Forms are actually the cause for the existence of all objects. Things are only said to exist insofar as they have order or structure or form.

Plato also points out that there is a hierarchy to Forms. Forms can interact to produce other Forms (such as geometrical Forms can combine to create the Form of a house). The theory of Forms is completed with the Form of Forms from which all those many Forms – the only true realities – must derive the characteristics which they themselves share. This supreme "Form of Good" comes to be along with so much else, the Form of the real also. The Forms are connected to each other and to material objects in an intricate system that reflects both the way they flow down from the Form of Good and the process that we must go through in working our way up to knowledge of the Forms. So the Forms flow down from the Form of Good going from most general, abstract, and objective (the Good) to most particular and subjective. All particular Forms are subsumed under more general Forms, and all Forms are finally subsumed under the Form of the Good. We work in the opposite direction and start from subjective concepts of the more particular things and work our way towards more objective concepts of the general, abstract Forms. The divided line represents the systematic interconnectedness of the Forms and how the advance of our knowledge reflects this system. The Form of Good is non-existent (non-physical) but bestows existence (physicality) upon things.

Mathematics and Our Universe

The so-called Pythagoreans, who were the first to take up mathematics, not only advanced this subject, but saturated with it, they fancied that the principles of mathematics were the principles of all things. – Aristotle, Metaphysics 1-5, cc. 350 BC

Over the entrance door to Plato's Academy, was the words "Let no one ignorant of geometry enter."

Physics is very much engaged in the mathematical behavior of matter, be it Newton's Laws or Quantum Mechanics or electrodynamics, etc. We have no understanding of why the universe operates according to some mathematical principles, but that appears to be inherently true; it is simply regarded as the properties of matter. However, can we go further than that? In 2007, by Max Tegmark, a Swedish-American cosmologist, who published scientific and popular articles on the Mathematical Universe Hypothesis (MUH) which states that our physical reality is a mathematical structure and that our universe is not just described by mathematics – it is mathematics.

"We don't invent mathematical structures – we discover them, and invent only the notation for describing them."

"We all live in a gigantic mathematical object – one that is more elaborate than a dodecahedron, and probably also more complex than objects with intimidating names like Calabi-Yau manifolds, tensor bundles, and Hilbert Space, which appear in today's most advanced theories. Everything in our world is mathematical – including you."

Tegmark's hypothesis seems to be surprisingly consistent with Pythagorean thinking.

Summary

The conclusions that we made at the beginning of this chapter about the pre-universe were made logically from what science could tell us about what was created at the Big Bang. This logical conclusion is consistent with the scientific nature of the vacuum energy of the universe. Both these conclusions were reached from knowledge of the outer world. Other cultures have reached this same knowledge by exploring our inner world of consciousness. It would appear that the pre-universe has been referred to by various names (dharmakaya, Ein Sof; The Tao, the Akashic Field, and Plato's Forms, to name a few). The "properties" of the pre-universe are: non-physical, unchanging and forever existing (having no time), omnipresent, and pure. From the point of view of physics, this would appear to be the "vacuum" of the universe, which is non-physical and present everywhere in the universe, but filled with virtual particles. From our subjective world, we have the dharmakaya, Ein Sof, Akashic Field, and Plato Forms. A "field" seems like a good term to use, in the same sense that we talk about a "field" of wheat. We mean this in a mathematical sense. We could say the pre-universe is a "field" populated with all kinds of physical potential, or Forms. Plato makes it clear that the non-physical abstract concepts (Forms) are outside of time as well, maintaining their "truth" forever. In addition, these Forms are pure, and are actually more real than our physical reality. In fact all these other terms mentioned refer to an experience of a greater reality than the physical reality, suggesting we have it backward. And remember, the pre-universe (by any name) is still with us.

These other terms, while consistent with the pre-universe, where all established long before the understanding of the Big Bang. This would mean that those who established these terms must have had a direct "experience" of the pre-universe. We would have to conclude that the pre-universe is connected with "consciousness" and may be pure consciousness, as suggested by those who have developed these terms. We have been told by Buddha, Lao Tzu, Jesus, Plato, to name a few, that it is possible to experience this state of "pre-universe," which is ever present. This is not a conclusion that scientists would reach about the "vacuum energy" of the universe, but they would have to admit that the pre-universe has the "potential" for consciousness, because "consciousness" has been actualized in the physical universe. If the pre-universe is "pure consciousness," then one could understand where the concept of "divine consciousness" and "cosmic consciousness" came from.

Intellectual knowledge and experiential knowledge are always quite different. The direct experience of the pre-universe is very different from the logical intellectual awareness of this knowledge.

DARK ENERGY AND THE SAMBOGAKAYA

Now, are we ready for the Big Bang? It would appear not yet. The pre-universe, or dharmakaya, would require a further step, before we can create a **physical** universe. The dharmakaya may have "too much information" to create an intelligible universe. Perhaps we need "rules" or "laws" or the right "patterns". These rules may be both physical laws and experiential laws. In Buddhism, the only thing that comes out of the dharmakaya (pre-universe) is the sambogakaya. This might be looked upon as a "filter" of sorts, allowing only what is necessary for this universe to exist. Now in Buddhism the sambogakaya is said to be made up of five basic "entities," which we could call Forms, but which Buddhism refers to as the Five Buddha Families, and which Taoists refer to as the Five Elements. This will be discussed in more detail in Chapter 4. But basically these are five "metaphorical" structures which experientially make up our entire objective and subjective world. They stand behind it and with all of it, much like Plato would describe his Forms. They are really abstract in nature. However, everything that we see or experience is ultimately made up of these 5 elements or Buddha Families, or Forms.

Dark Energy is a hypothetical form of energy that permeates all of space and tends to accelerate the expansion of the universe. Physicists today are uncertain what Dark Energy is – they believe that it makes up about 68.3% of the mass/energy of the universe. Perhaps Dark Energy acts like a filter, limiting what types of virtual particles which exist in the vacuum energy, to actually manifest in this physical universe. It would seem that the sambogakaya (or dark energy?) must exist before matter comes into existence. Dark Energy seems to be creating the "space" for the universe, and this suggests that the creation of the universe is an ongoing event. Perhaps the explosion hasn't stopped.

DARK MATTER AND THE NIRMANAKAYA

So, are we ready for the Big Bang? Almost. If one takes a look at the knowledge of mysticism (which will be discussed in more detail in the next chapter), the creation of matter begins with subtle matter, eventually culminating in the dense matter of our present visible matter. As we have discussed, we have concluded that subtle matter is dark matter. But we cannot say exactly how many layers of "subtle matter" exist. However, the last form of matter created, the densest, is what scientists refer to as the Big Bang. That's when elementary particles come into being, such as protons, neutrons, and electrons, and eventually atoms of charge, which make up the periodic table, come into being.

To keep it simple, after the creation of "dark energy," we have the creation of a series of subtle matters (dark matters). Using the system of Hinduism the series could be:

1. Ananda-energy (equivalent to the sambogakaya, or dark energy?)
2. Vijnana-matter
3. Mano-matter
4. Prana-matter
5. Anna-matter (visible matter, electrically charged matter, the elements of the periodic table)

Of course, there could be more forms of subtle matter, but these are the basic divisions. So the last type of matter to be created in this scenario, is our visible matter – and this is, at last, the Big Bang, which occurred about 13.82 billion years ago.

CONCLUSION

From the point of view of mysticism, and from the point of view of modern science, the universe was formed out of an eternal, nonphysical "entity," which we refer to as the pre-universe, which could be called the dharmakaya, or the Ein Sof, or the Tao, or the Akashic Field, or the Elysian Field, or God the Father, or Plato's Forms, or the Vacuum Energy. These terms all seem to ultimately refer to the same pre-universe. This eternal pre-universe contains no physical objects, but contains the potential for the existence of physical objects. Furthermore, the pre-universe being outside of time, still exists, and is unchangeable (you can't add anything to it or take anything away from it). It is intriguing that physicists have been so successful in chasing down the basic laws governing the behavior of the physical universe, but have not asked "**where** do these physical laws (or any scientific principles) exist?" The ultimate laws or principles of the universe are not physical themselves, even though they may be eternal (as true today as they were before they were discovered). To change our focus from the universe to the "place" where these laws or principles exist, might prove even more valuable than the principles themselves.

To create a physical universe, we need a "blueprint," or a set of principles around which the universe can manifest. As mentioned, this would be the sambogakaya, which we believe is what physicists call dark energy. This is the essence which is causing the physical universe to expand at an ever increasing rate. This "dark energy" may be responsible for creating "relative space" for the universe, from the beginning to the present. The expansion hasn't stopped. Also, the sambogakaya is the domain of the five basic metaphorical "elements" or five buddha families.

Next we have the creation of dark matter or subtle matter. There could be numerous types of subtle matter - it is difficult to know how western physics might eventually categorize them. This creation of subtle matters eventually culminates in the creation of visible matter, which is the Big Bang event.

The actual experience of the entire nirmanakaya would lead one to the direct experience of the sambogakaya, and then the dharmakaya.

In our usual state of being we are separate beings – we could say we are many. In the sambogakaya we are one. The dharmakaya is beyond logic, even though it provides the potential for logic (and everything else) in the physical universe. In the dharmakaya we cannot say if we are one or many.

CHAPTER 4

THE SCIENCE OF CORRESPONDENCE:

TRADITIONAL APPROACHES TO

SPIRITUAL EXPERIENCES

PRELIMINARY REMARKS

We are all aware of the rituals, rites, ceremonies, chants, mantras, symbols, iconography, altars, mythic stories, etc. utilized in spirituality, but typically we don't understand the reason, purpose, meaning, technique or value, of these activities. In this chapter we will explore these forms of metaphorical thinking as a powerful tool for experiencing mystical knowledge. In mysticism, the metaphorical process provides a surprising path to deep experiences. This is how we get there.

We must first understand the vast difference between intellectual knowledge and experiential knowledge. Consider the following. We live in a contradiction of astronomical proportions. On the one hand we are one individual in a planet of several billion people, in a solar system that is one of billions in the Milky Way, which in turn is one of 170 billion galaxies in the universe. This scientifically provable fact makes us seemingly insignificant. On the other hand we are the only consciousness we can experience, and we are the center from which our consciousness views this universe. This obvious experiential fact makes us the center of our universe. So which are we? Well, no one would question that we are obviously both. One is a scientific logical perspective, the other an experiential perspective.

In viewing "time" one finds a similar contradiction. From the point of view of Western science, the present moment is but an instant in the spectrum of time, a time which begins with the big bang extends to the present and far into the distant future. However, experientially the present moment is eternal, all there is, all we can ever know. The past is but a memory experienced in the present moment, and the future is an expectation experienced in the present moment. All our knowledge of the past is determined through the present moment, whether it's through memory, books, experiments, whatever, it is all knowledge experienced in the present moment. The future is a projection of this moment. We cannot go physically back in time even one second to see if the universe existed then – we can only presume it existed through the knowledge that the eternally present experiential moment gives us. These simple examples demonstrate the difference between experience knowledge and intellectual knowledge.

We should also note that when discussing the phenomenal world we share (our common reality), logic can be utilized for understanding this world. However, when we are discussing experiences which we do not have in common, which others have not shared, logic cannot direct others to these experiences, and one must depend upon analogy and metaphor to represent this other world, this other experience. For example, what we experience as an adult can at best only be explained through analogy to a child. Amazingly enough, as we will see, metaphors can be employed which have an exact representation to the deeper concepts of interest. Mystical teachings exclusively utilize these types of powerful metaphors.

While present day Western science is based on logical connections leading to an intellectual comprehension of the universe, a science based on analogical or metaphorical connections can be and has been developed, which leads one to an experiential understanding of the universe. The concept of science can and should be generalized to include any natural connection the human mind makes between concepts. Swedenborg referred to this metaphorical science as the "science of correspondence." Mysticism has utilized this broader definition of science, and in so doing has developed a basis for teaching and communicating their discoveries and understandings. We have already demonstrated that the recent Western scientific discovery of dark matter is consistent with mystical findings of subtle bodies and various "planes of matter" or consciousness. Here we will show that traditional mystical metaphorical connections can form the basis of the path toward experiencing our subtle bodies, and thus toward our spiritual growth.

THE SCIENCE OF CORRESPONDENCE

"The perfect transformation of that blind world-creating urge into the force of liberation, depends on the perfection of inner vision, on the universality of inner knowledge. By becoming conscious of the world and of those forces which create it, we become their master. As long as these forces remain dormant and unperceived within us, we have no access to them. For this reason it is necessary to project them into the realm of the visible in the form of images. The symbols which serve this purpose act like a chemical catalyst, through which a liquid is suddenly converted into solid crystals, thus revealing its true nature and structure." – *Lama Anagarika Govinda,* Foundations of Tibetan Mysticism

As David V. Tansley points out, "although a basic intellectual understanding of the subtle bodies is important, this mode of knowing must be transcended and transformed into experience; this alone turns the key to the locked door of the

Mysteries and provides the student with a true knowledge of his inner being."[48]

One may wonder how it is that other cultures, in particular mystical cultures and third world cultures, have developed an awareness of subtle bodies. One may also wonder how one might become aware of subtle bodies. Or one may wonder how Western science must be generalized to include mystical understandings. Well the answer to all these questions may lie in our natural thinking processes. Mystics as well as third world cultures think more often metaphorically, whereas the Western scientific world is dominated by logical thinking. And it is through the metaphorical or analogical thinking process that, it appears, the key to the locked doors is turned. **Apparently "metaphor" is the vehicle which provides the power for direct experience of subtler levels of consciousness.**

This may give insight into why Western science techniques have been so successful in exploring the physical universe. The best suggestion might be that scientific thought can be based on <u>precise</u> connections utilized naturally by the human mind. So for example, when we utilize <u>precise</u> <u>logical</u> connections we develop our Western science. But since the human mind can think and connect in other ways as well, such as analogically or metaphorically, it would therefore seem reasonable that <u>precise</u> <u>analogical</u> connections could also be developed into a science. The determinant factor for creating a science may not be dependent upon the <u>type</u> of mental connection, but rather the <u>precision</u> of the mental connection. Poor logic obviously leads to an inaccurate conclusion, as would a bad analogy.

When we generalize our definition of science in this way, then it becomes clear that some ancient cultures, some third world cultures, mystics and shamans, have already developed an analogical or metaphorical science, which Emanuel Swedenborg called the "science of correspondence" (an excellent term for this science). Swedenborg referred to this science as the "Science of Sciences," but it could also be called the "Art of Arts." Indeed, this metaphorical thinking is closer to Western arts (music, poetry, painting, dance, etc.) than to our Western sciences. Although Swedenborg believed that this metaphorical science was very well known by advanced ancient cultures and had mostly been lost, he did not have available to him the literature or beliefs of much of the world, of Tibet, China, India, Japan, Africa, or the shamans of the American Indians or the Australian Aborigines.

The science of correspondence is more than an analogical or metaphorical way of organizing information. A true metaphor as used here contains the potential for an *identity* between the object and the symbol. Not all analogies have this quality. But this identity is not readily apparent in our normal state of consciousness. A significant change in our state of mind is required in order to experience the relationship as an identity. Joseph Campbell equates this state of consciousness to the opening of the Heart chakra. The techniques associated with the science of correspondence can allow this shift of consciousness, in time, to occur.

The science of correspondence has an aesthetic quality to it, is inclusive of all systems, is humbling, often appearing simple and naïve from our Western point of view, and tends toward long term solutions and a quality of patience. While Western science is primarily logical in nature, the true spiritual perspective is primarily metaphorical in nature. Swedenborg believed that the hieroglyphics and the entire ancient Egyptian language where based on spiritual correspondences, as was the original writing of the Bible. In this context it is of interest to consider Joseph Campbell's statement that, "God can be understood as a metaphor for a mystery which transcends all categories of human thought." Here it would appear that these metaphors can produce spiritual truths, just as logic can produce scientific truths.

This analogical science is quite unlike our Western logical science. It takes us in a different direction and yields unique information about the nature of mankind and the universe. In essence, the science of correspondence appears to be more experiential in nature, producing direct knowledge of that which is being studied. This presents an apparent conflict with Western science – a difficult hurdle to overcome, since Western science is intellectual in nature, believing that intellectual understandings are supreme and free of bias or superstition, and does not in the least trust direct experiential or intuitive knowing. In fact the only statement traditional Western science has made about experience is "don't trust it." Although the end pursuit of Western science appears to be an intellectual comprehension of the universe, the science of mysticism is primarily involved with a direct knowledge of some ultimate reality, experience, etc., a knowledge or wisdom which cannot be comprehended intellectually, and therefore MUST BE DIRECTLY EXPERIENCED. It's a journey we must ultimately make on our own, preferably with experienced teachers to guide us, for it is not without risks.

Simply stated, the science of correspondence is a functional metaphorical/analogical relationship between two logically unrelated objects or events. At a deeper level of consciousness, this *relationship* becomes an *identity*. This has to be experienced, and cannot be intellectually grasped. The science of correspondence requires a long-term investigation in order to be comprehended and utilized properly, just as does our Western science. If you combine Carl Jung's concepts of "synchronicity" and "archetypes," you will find something very much like the science of correspondence. This analogical or metaphorical science is applied in mythology, iconography, true ritual and ceremony, dreams, as well as in alchemy, astrology, the Kabbalah, and mystical symbology. An excellent example of correspondence is the Mandala, a symbol utilized by many cultures, and which corresponds to man and to the universe. Obviously this is not a physical description or drawing of man or of the universe, nor is it just an informative symbolic representation, but the Mandala is a precise correspondence to man and to the universe. The practice of these disciplines is best explored with a highly qualified teacher, which is often difficult to find and difficult to recognize. However, the study of any of these systems can potentially lead to a nonpredictable, nonlogical, mysterious change in consciousness which puts one in touch with a "greater reality."

Meditation

To begin with, we should mention meditation, which is usually a prerequisite and a co-requisite for spiritual development. In fact some practices, such as sadhanas, are useless until one has reached a certain level of meditative skill. Practiced since antiquity, one can view some meditation practices as mental disciplines designed to perhaps promote relaxation, or develop compassion or love or other virtues, or perhaps to develop internal energy (qi), or possibly with no particular goal in mind. There is such a variety of meditative practices that one could easily write volumes on the subject. So in this book we will simply mention the need for this basic discipline in whatever form it takes.

Some sophisticated studies have been made on EEG (electroencephalography) patterns recorded along the scalp on individual during meditation. Typically, these EEG patterns are divided into 4 major groups:

Alpha (8-13Hz) – Alert, relaxed waking consciousness
Beta (13-30 Hz) – Alert, sometimes agitated waking
consciousness
Theta (4-8 Hz) – Dream state and sometimes states of
creativity
Delta (up to 4 Hz) – Deep sleep state (in-between dream state)

Typically, people who have developed meditative skills perhaps after 20 years of practice, can move into different states of consciousness at will, and show different EEG patterns. Some meditators have demonstrated the ability to drop these wave patterns to essentially zero, a profound brain change. These meditative skills are equivalent to the control of gross bodily functions which some yogis have demonstrated. Different brain wave patterns indicate different states of consciousness. For example, a skilled meditator in a deep delta wave pattern of sleep who is also producing alpha wave patterns, they report being in a lucid dream state (a dream state in which one is aware that one is dreaming). Of course you cannot reduce meditative states to brain states – they have different qualities to them, but they can be correlated.

Symbology

"The rationalists of the eighteenth century, or the historical materialists of the nineteenth century, were of the opinion that mankind in its intellectual development had transcended the symbol; today we not only admit the continuing force of symbolic modes of thought, but are even compelled to make a plea for their revival and extension." – Herbert Read, The Forms of Things Unknown.

Man communicates through symbols. Whether those symbols are the spoken word, the written word, pictures or images, they are still symbols and are not the object or concept itself. We cannot directly transfer experiences from one individual to another. We cannot simultaneously share our experiences – we can only share events. We can point to a tree or the grass or the sky, but we cannot know how the other person experiences these things, so they are symbols also – symbols of themselves. Symbols come in various shapes and sizes, have various connotations, and are more or less significant or meaningful. A symbol can be representational, codified, analogical, etc. But visual or verbal symbols in mysticism are not just representational or codified or analogical but convey a basic identity with the object or concept they symbolize. That is to say they connect in a pure objective sense, but not necessarily in a logical sense. They can be experienced as an identity, the symbol and that which is symbolized. This type of "correspondent" symbology is used in all techniques which lead to a mystical or spiritual understanding of the universe and of mankind. Let us explore this further.

Dreams

"Sometimes dreams are wiser than waking." – Black Elk – Holy Man of the Oglala Sioux

Dreams are the personal aspect of myth. Dreams and their meaning seem to get rediscovered, and it was Freud who rediscovered the value of dreams in the 20th Century. "In 1900, Sigmund Freud published in Vienna a voluminous work on the analysis of dreams. Here are the principle results of his investigation. The dream, far from being the confusion of haphazard and meaningless associations it is commonly believed to be, or a result merely of somatic sensations during sleep as many authors suppose, is an autonomous and meaningful product of psychic activity, susceptible, like all other psychic functions, of a systematic analysis. The organic sensations felt during sleep are not the cause of the dream; they play but a secondary role and furnish only elements (the material) upon which the psyche works. According to Freud the dream, like every complex psychic product, is a creation, a piece of work which has its motives, its trains of antecedent associations; and like any considered action it is the outcome of a logical process, of the competition between various tendencies and the victory of one tendency over another. Dreaming has meaning like everything else we do. It may be objected that all empirical reality is against this theory, since the impression of incoherence and obscurity that dreams make upon us is notorious. Freud calls this sequence of confused images the *manifest content* of the dream; it is the facade behind which he looks for what is essential – namely, the dream-thought or the *latent content.* ... Freud applies to the dream the same principle that we always instinctively use when inquiring into the causes of human actions. He asks himself quite simple: why does this particular person dream this particular thing?"[49]

An earlier scientist who utilized dreams in his exploration of the inner world was Emanuel Swedenborg. His personal approach to the language of correspondence began with the symbols that appeared in his dreams. In 1744 he was completing his four volumes of the brain which threw light on the operations of the brain and were appreciated only centuries later. But still not being able to find the soul in man, he pursued an inward journey, utilizing his dreams. Instead of just occasionally jotting down dreams, he began to record and interpret them daily. "Eventually Swedenborg's feeling and imagery burst forth, presenting symbols within symbols growing, comprehending all." After a very long process of self-analysis and inner changes which he inadvertently undertook in this process, the visionary tendency broke into his waking life. He later stated, "We must not, by our own power and by own intelligence, begin to doubt the heavenly truths which are revealed to us." Swedenborg said that he was permitted to walk in heaven and hell, and allowed to write extensively about these experiences.[50]

Carl Jung states that, "The dream is a little hidden door in the innermost and most secret recesses of the soul, opening into that cosmic night which was psyche long before there was any ego consciousness, and which will remain psyche no matter how far our ego-consciousness extends. For all ego-consciousness is isolated; because it separates and discriminates, it knows only particulars, and it sees only those that can be related to the ego. Its essence is limitation, even though it reaches to the farthest nebulae among the stars. All consciousness separates; but in dreams we put on the likeness of that more universal, truer, more eternal man dwelling in the darkness of primordial night. There he is still the whole, and the whole is in him, indistinguishable from nature and bare of all egohood."[51]

Arnold Mindell, who developed Process Oriented Psychology, discovered that the information dreams convey can be also of a bodily nature. He states that, "All your dreams manifest as body experiences which eventually turn into symptoms if you don't work on them very much. The physical occurrence may not manifest right away as a symptom."[52]

To explain this process, Mindell develops the concept of the dreambody, which he equates to the subtle bodies: "I define the concept of the dreambody as body experiences which we have, which we feel. When we feel in great depth and experiment with our feelings and amplify those feelings, this phenomena about the experiences in our bodies are mirrored in our dreams. I call that the dreambody. For example, if you have migraine headaches that you experience as poundings and you then go ahead and investigate the experience and the feeling of pounding, you might suddenly feel that there's a lot of drums pounding and people are about ready to fight one another — in an ordinary state of consciousness. You just investigate the feelings of your body, a migraine, and you see drummers and feel the pounding of your head — and suddenly you remember, Oh my God, I dreamt the other night that there was a war going on. So this phenomena of body experiences mirroring what you have dreamt, this is what I call the dreambody. It means that all body problems, all body symptoms are dreams trying to manifest through the body. ... Everybody thinks that the body is bad and the body is pathological ... and that when you're sick, it's something to cure, instead of seeing that when you're sick, that's some energy trying to happen that could be very useful to you and to everybody else, not just to yourself and your own personal growth."[53] One could say that illness, sickness, pain and aches are correspondences to something greater, often revealed through dreams.

Despite the vast information on dreams presented by Freud, Jung, Mindell and many others, scientists still tend to view dreams as meaningless fantasies, and all too many non-scientists want to view dreams as being somehow prophetic. Dreams cannot be reduced so easily.

Dream symbolism is a good example of the science of correspondence at work. One has to wonder if the symbolism of dreams is not "literal" in a deeper sense, and only seems like complex symbols from our limited state on mind in this limited existence.

Chakras

Symbolism used for the chakras are not meant to be physical drawings of the chakras, but are symbolic correspondences. Also, the chakras have a psychodynamic correspondence. One can say that the first chakra equates to survival, the second to reproduction, and the third to power. Joseph Campbell points out that when people are living on the levels of the first three chakras they are living on the animal level. Animals too cling to life, animals too propagate, animals too fight to win. When we are living on this level we have to be controlled by social law — dharma. Our popular religions, says Campbell, are concerned with prayers for health, wealth, prodigy, and victory. "We are not in the field of true religious life, in the field of the spiritual birth, until we have come up to chakra four. And this is at the level of the heart, the sacred heart, Anahata — that means 'not hit.'"[54] What this refers to, says Campbell, is the sound that's not made of any two things not striking together, which is "OM" (AUM); it is the sound of the energy of the universe of which all things are manifestations. This is the midpoint of transcendence, to realization. This is the level of the breakthrough of the metaphysical level **that the two that seem to be separate are really one. While in our normal state of mind relationship appears separate, here we can experience that relationship becomes identity (seeing the identity in the correspondence); we can experience the self-luminous bodies (which are the subtle bodies).** Here the first three chakras fall into a secondary position.

Further, Campbell says, at the throat chakra, Visuddha — purgation — we have the sublimation of the animal physical experience, the turning about of the shakti. At the Ajna, or position between the eyes, which deals with authority, power on the spiritual level, the soul beholds its object. At the crown chakra we have the thousand-petaled lotus, where one has the experience of "I and the Father are One."[55]

Mythology

"The palace of the Sun rose up in columns Of flaming gold and brass: ivory the ceiling, And double palace doors were bright as mirrors In silver light, and yet more valuable Than gold and silver was the craft that made them." From Ovid's Metamorphoses, Phaethon's Ride

In the nineteenth century scholars mostly treated myths with the usual meaning of the word, such as "false," "fiction," "invention." In the 20th Century we find Western scholars who have approached the study of myth markedly different, "they have accepted it as it was understood in the archaic societies, where, on the contrary, 'myth' means 'true story' and, beyond that, a story that is a most precious possession because it is sacred, exemplary, significant. This new semantic value given to the term 'myth' makes its use in contemplary parlance somewhat equivocal. Today, that is, the word is employed both in the sense of 'fiction' or 'illusion' and in that familiar especially to ethnologists, sociologists, and historians of religions, the sense of sacred tradition, primordial revelation, exemplary model."[56]

Joseph Campbell says that, "throughout the inhabited world, in all times and under every circumstance, the myths of man have flourished; and they have been the living inspiration of whatever else may have appeared out of the activities of the human mind. It would not be too much to say that myth is the secret opening through which the inexhaustible energies of the cosmos pour into human cultural manifestation. Religions, philosophies, arts, the social forms of primitive and historic man, prime discoveries in science and technology, the very dreams that blister sleep, boil up from the basic, magic ring of myth."[57] Joseph Campbell, brought mythology to the forefront in the Western world as no one else had, and has shown us that mythology is a method of utilizing theater or storytelling to connect with a deeper reality, and allow us to experience that reality. Mythological thinking is a metaphor or "correspondence" to a much greater world. By exploring these stories, one can begin to experience the correspondence of this imagery.

Mudras

A mudra is a gesture made with the hands that expresses an idea, emotion, or object. Hand gestures and positioning of these types are used in rituals and iconography of all religions. Some typical mudras commonly used in depictions of the Buddha are (a) the dhyana mudra which is depicted with palms up and thumbs in front, represents the posture of the Buddha as he meditates, (b) the abhaya mudra, or fear-not posture, which has one palm facing forward and fingers pointing up as he dispels the fears of his followers, and (c) the varada mudra, with palm facing forward and fingers down, portraying divine blessing. Some mudras can also include movements of the wrists, elbows, and shoulders. "Most of these mudras are formed as variations on four basic hand positions: flat palm, cupped palm, closed fist, and fingers and thumb together. Indian treatises have classified 32 major hand positions with about 500 different meanings. These gestures represent gods, demons, emperors, flowers (there are more than 60 lotus flower mudras), rivers, mountains, sunsets, birds, and such feelings as love, wonder, surprise, worry, and hate."[58]

One can find hand gestures in all religions during rituals. Although the mudra can represent externally the meaning presented by the mudra, mudras are more than representational symbols; they are correspondences. By utilizing the mudra, one can obtain an inner experience of the meaning of these hand symbols.

Body Postures

The power of the "positioning" of the body is often overlooked by the Western culture. A few examples are: (a) in qigong, the wu chi posture utilized is very important to enable the individual to maximize the experience provided by these qi exercises, as are the numerous tai chi chuan postures; (b) in Yoga, the lotus posture (padmasana) is utilized for meditation, and numerous asanas are practiced for health, relaxation, and spiritual growth; (c) in Tibet, there are specific postures to aid one in experiencing the 5 Buddha Families (basic energies).

Felicitas D. Goodman in her book *Where the Spirits Ride the Wind* discusses the utilization of different body postures by cultures throughout the world as a door to opening certain experiences. There are body postures which can be utilized for healing, for out-of-body-experiences, for visions, for prayer, for spirit journeys, for divining, etc. She provides numerous accounts of individual experiences initiated through postures employed by various cultures for these purposes.[59] For this reason, body postures are frequently used as part of rituals as well.

These experiences demonstrate the power of specific body postures as correspondences, allowing the individual to enter into certain experiences induced by the power of the posture.

Altars and Object Arrangement

Altars are a sacred arrangement of objects that provide a meaningful correspondence of import to the community and/or the individual. The arrangement of objects allows the profane to become sacred. Altars can be made in a religious setting, such as a church, temple, house of worship, sacred place, or in one's home. They provide a focus for ceremonies and rituals. From time immemorial mankind has used meaningful objects, such as amulets, candles, holy water, incense, crystals, icons, nature objects, gems, etc., to provide a point of comfort, a connection between the visible and spiritual worlds.

Individuals often instinctively create their own altars. Artist Barbara Kazanis notes that, "I had an enormous number of special little objects that I arranged around my house in groupings. I moved them often and 'played' with them. It now occurred to me that they resembled small altars, the kind where we place important remembrances, prayers, wishes, losses, and the mysterious tears we either haven't shed or are now shedding and need to acknowledge – small altars where we are able to be present to deep feelings and meanings for a moment or two because we are able to focus and feel connected to something deeper and bigger than ourselves, making it safe to open our hearts and really be present for the moment – small altars where things that felt solid and immoveable seem spontaneously to begin to shimmer and move and where a certain ease of breath comes to us."[60] She went on to utilize the making of altars, or the arrangement of objects, to aid individuals to heal by connecting the personal with the universal.

Rites, Rituals and Ceremonies

"What happened next is the kind of experience that ... molded my perception forever. The tree that I had been watching for so long was no longer there, and in its place was a beautiful green lady ... Where the tree had been there was now a figure that looked like a human being, in the shape of a women, very tall, probably seven and a half feet tall. ... I do not know how I knew this, but this green was the expression of immeasurable love." – Malidoma Patrice Some, The Healing Wisdom of Africa

Rituals and ceremonies typically employ many methods of correspondence, including movement, gestures, body postures, mantras, mudras, prayers, chants, etc., in the presence of icons, altars, and other symbolic representations, in an effort to bring forth a "quality" or "presence" or a deeper reality one is connecting with, perhaps as a re-enactment of a spiritual event, usually for the purposes of healing and/or spiritual growth. Rituals can last from minutes to weeks.

One could say that there are two parts to a ritual. One part is planned by the people performing the ritual, and the other part cannot be planned, and is a spontaneous, almost unpredictable interaction with an energy source.

A central ritual in Christian theology, the ritual of the sacrament of the Eucharist, is utilized in transubstantiation (a doctrine that says that, the bread and wine become the actual body and blood of Jesus Christ). Transubstantiation is opposed to other doctrines, such as consubstantiation, that assert that the body and blood of Christ coexist with the bread and wine, which remain unchanged. The doctrine of transubstantiation was reconfirmed by the Council of Trent (1551) and restated by Pope Paul VI in 1965. Transubstantiation is a doctrine of the Roman Catholic Church and the Orthodox Church.

The roots of this word "trans" and "substance" indicates the possibility of a more general usage of the term "transubstantiation." Today, however, it exclusively refers to the *identity* of bread and wine to the body and blood of Christ. So here we have another major example in spirituality of this *identity* between the symbol and that which it symbolizes.

Today, a technique referred to as "expressive arts," utilizes the quality of the arting experience to bring forth, when performed properly, a deep quality of humankind, much like authentic rituals do.

Chinese movements, such as qigong and tai chi also have this quality of ritual enactment.

Astrology

The relationship of the stars to mankind is certainly ancient in nature. We have discussed earlier how astrology may physically operate through the subtle bodies, but the astrological chart of an individual is also a correspondence to that individual. Through the process of observing the integration of the energies of the planets through the qualities of the astrological signs as well as the planetary angular aspects, a complex understanding of the nature of the individual and the universe unfolds. By reading astrological charts one begins to see the interaction of universal events through these basic energies. If applied successfully, this could eventually lead to an experiential understanding of these energies and also the operation of the basic alchemical elements.

Kabbalah

Recently, great interest has developed in the Kabbalah, and significant information has been made available. "The term Kabbalah translates literally into tradition, and refers us specifically to the tradition of Jewish mysticism."[61] It is based on traditional literature of the Jewish Religion, such as the Torah, the Talmud, Mishna, Gemara, Midrash, Halakhah and Aggadah.

Although seemingly complex to comprehend, the understanding of this system as a science of correspondence aids in its discernment. The Sephirothic Tree can correspond to any situation, and an understanding of this complex symbol and how to properly apply it is a central theme in the Kabbalah. There are 10 sephiroth in the Sephirothic Tree and they are regarded as abstract entities through which all changes take place. The 10 sephiroth are connected by 32 paths (of wisdom). Every aspect of life can be categorized into one or more of the 10 sephiroth.

This Sephirothic Tree is like a template which must be skillfully laid upon life situations. The skill is in fully understanding the correspondences so that the system can be applied properly, and this takes a lot of patience, effort, and practice. At first one must perform careful analysis, translating each situation appropriately, but in time, much like learning a foreign language, there comes a day when one does not need to translate, and one grasps the correspondence immediately.

Herbalogy

Herbs are utilized by all cultures from China to Africa to India to the North and South America. Our relationship with plants and their properties is universal. Herbalogy is generally regarded as the utilization of plants for nutritional or medicinal purposes, but herbalogy includes ceremonial plants as well, which can be utilized in sacred rituals.

In the west, numerous pharmaceuticals are obtained from plants – penicillin was obtained from a fungus in 1928. Clinical research is continuing to document the health-giving benefits from select fungi/mushrooms. And although herbalogy was traditionally ignored by Western medicine, today you can find courses on medical herbalogy.

Herbal remedies have become a big business in the West. Although active ingredients have been extracted from some herbal remedies, others have failed to produce an active ingredient and some have several. Extracting the active ingredient can produce a pharmaceutical agent that often produces side effects which the herbal remedy did not. It appears that there is a synergistic effect of the herbal remedy which eliminates or significantly reduces any side effects.

We have only scratched the surface of herbal remedies. There are claims by many cultures of having actual cures for ailments which we in the West can at best only keep under control (such as diabetes and high blood pressure).

One may wonder how herbal remedies where discovered. It was not through the techniques of Western scientific research, but through the science of correspondence. In China, this involves a holistic perspective of the world, and such concepts as Yin and Yang, and the five basic elements. For example, herbs are regarded as having four natures: cold, hot, warm and cool; five tastes: spicy, sour, sweet, bitter and salty; four actions: ascending, descending, floating and sinking. These qualities can be related to the corresponding nature of the disease to determine which herbs to use, a very complex, integrated system.

In some cases, the "law of signatures" can be utilized where the shape and/or color and/or smell and/or taste of the plant is utilized as related to the symptoms of the individual. On a simple level a particular kidney shaped bean may be useful for kidney ailments, and a specific yellow plant or flower might be useful for jaundice.

Alchemy

Carl Jung has written considerably upon the subject of alchemy, exploring the incredible images presented to the world through this system. As an analyst he found great value in the structure and source of these rich symbols, and utilized them accordingly. Carl Jung discovered "how certain archetypal motifs that are common in alchemy appear in the dreams of modern individuals who have no knowledge of alchemical literature."[62] He demonstrated that "the wealth of ideas and symbols that lie hidden in the neglected treatises of this much misunderstood 'art' definitely does not belong to the rubbish heap of the past, but stands in a very real and living relationship to our most recent discoveries concerning the psychology of the unconscious. Not only does this modern psychological discipline give us the key to the secrets of alchemy, but, conversely, alchemy provides the psychology of the unconscious with a meaningful historical basis. This is hardly a popular subject, and for that reason it remained largely misunderstood. Not only was alchemy almost entirely unknown as a branch of natural philosophy and as a religious movement, but most people were unfamiliar with the modern discovery of the archetypes, or had at least misunderstood them."[63]

Alchemy seems to hold such contradictory information that one finds logic and common sense of limited value. It is a journey, a path. All of our present day sciences grew out of Alchemy – our chemistry, physics, medicine, astronomy, etc., had their birth in Alchemy. Newton himself was a great explorer of alchemy and spent much more time in this subject then he did on the traditional Western sciences.

Despite Carl Jung's understanding, appreciation and writings on alchemy, and Newton's great interest, today mainstream scientists still view alchemy only as an ancient attempt to understand the world, but one that was incorrect and has no place in the world today. In our scientific textbooks, no mention is made of Jung's understanding of alchemy, but it is only stated that this is what primitive man incorrectly believed.

Carl Jung showed how the images and processes utilized by alchemists could be seen as paths to psychological transformations. But they go beyond that, even. The words and images utilized by the alchemists are easily misunderstood because, again, we have to think in metaphorical terms. For example, a basic metaphor in mysticism is the five "element" theory. But the use of the word "element" here is not at all the way we use the term "element" in Western science today. What is meant here is something more fundamental, more elemental, then the dense physical elements of our modern science. The alchemist's/mystic's elements are fundamental from a metaphorical perspective. These "elements" are the basic "metaphorical elements" of the universe. The alchemist's "elements" can be seen in the physical and emotional and mental and spiritual aspects of man and the universe, i.e. all levels of consciousness as well as the dense physical universe. That is to say, it is present in all the bodies, subtle and dense, and all "planes of matter," subtle and dense, metaphorically. The term is used to represent the 5 basic qualities of both the objective and subjective universe. That is, the 5 "element" theory needs to be understood through the Swedenborg's science of correspondence or analogical/metaphorical science, and not through logical science.

In eastern thought we find 5 basis elements: "earth," "water," "fire," "air," and "space." In Buddhism the elements are personified into the Five Buddha Families: *buddha, vajra, padma, ratna, and karma families.* Although each Buddha Family is associated with an "element," one or more of the Buddha Families can be used to describe a person's basic interaction with or approach to the world. Each Buddha Family principle can have a confused and enlightened expression, as the particular "neurosis" associated with a *buddha* family can be transmuted into its enlightened aspect.

For example, in the *buddha* family the basic "element" or quality is space, which is all-encompassing and open in nature. Space can provide a vessel in which all the other qualities can interact or mingle. Subjectively, the confused quality of this family is one of ignorance in the sense of ignoring or avoiding, not wanting to see. In the enlightened state, this quality manifests as *the wisdom of all-encompassing space.* It is associated with the color white, its direction is the center, and is symbolized by a wheel, representing this open quality.

For the *vajra* family, the basic "element" is water, an energy that tends to flow downward. The basic quality of the *vajra* family relates to intellectual ability, which can view situations from many perspectives, able to see the whole picture as well as the details. In the confused state, one is angry, aggressive or intellectually fixated. It is much like the world of academia. The enlightened form is *mirror-like wisdom*, a quality of sharp, clear reflectiveness. It is associated with the color blue, the direction east, and symbolized by a vajra scepter, which represents a diamond-like quality of indestructibility.

For the *ratna* family, the basic "element" is earth, which has the qualities of solidness, inertia, as well as fertility. The basic quality here is one of richness. In the confused state, there is a sense of pride; one can be very self-indulgent, enjoying leisure and comfort, which can become envy or hunger, desiring everything. Being proud, you may feel yourself constantly challenged by the possibility of failure and defeat. In the enlightened state it becomes the *wisdom of equanimity,* accommodating all experiences and bringing out their innate richness. It is represented by the color yellow (gold), the direction south, and symbolized by a jewel, which represents richness.

For the *padma* family, the basic "element" is fire, which has an upward, consuming movement like flames. Its basic quality is passion. On a confused level this passion can become grasping or clinging, and like fire, it does not distinguish between those things it grasps, burns or destroys. It ignores the real state of being united and wants to possess in order to become united. In the enlightened state, it becomes *discriminating-awareness wisdom,* the warmth of compassion, which appreciates every aspect of experience. It is represented by the color red, the direction west, and symbolized by a lotus, a beautiful pure flower which grows out of muddy waters.

For the *karma* family, the basic "element" is air or wind, characterized by a tendency to revolve in different directions and to relate itself to other possibilities. Its basic quality is action, always eager to start something new, always busy but efficient. The confused state of this family is excessive speed and resentment, particularly of any disorder or inefficiency. One feels that one is not going to achieve any of one's goals, and become irritated with the accomplishment of others. The *karma* quality in the enlightened state becomes the *wisdom of all-accomplishing action,* able to accomplish one's goals with appropriate energy, without resentment. It is represented by the color green, the direction north, and symbolized by a sword, which cuts through hesitation.

The idea here is not one of manipulation or of judgment, but to simply see or experience the world as the interplay of five "elements" or Five Buddha Family qualities. Thus learning to observe these basic qualities of the universe at work in the world, in situations, in people, is a great spiritual exercise, leading eventually (hopefully) to the enlightened aspects of these qualities.

Holy Trinity and the Trikaya Doctrine

Understanding or experiencing the five basic elements can potentially open one up to the experience of the Holy Trinity (in Christianity) or the Trikaya Doctrine of Buddhism. The Father, Son and Holy Spirit correlate with the Dharmakaya, the Sambhogakaya (body of bliss), and the Nirmanakaya of Buddhism. These sacred doctrines are very difficult to explain verbally, but do represent a very high level spiritual experience. The approach to these concepts is quite unique for each religion. These doctrines have been represented in the iconography of religions, but still remain quite mysterious.

Lama Anagarika Govinda states that: "every Buddha manifests himself on three planes of reality: the universal, the ideal and the individual. Thus we discern in the figure of the Buddha three 'bodies' or principles: (1) that, in which all Enlightened Ones are the same: the experience of completeness, of universality, of the deepest super-individual reality of the Dharma, the primordial law and cause of all things, from which emanates all physical, moral and metaphysical order; (2) that which constitutes the spiritual or ideal character of a Buddha, the creative expression or formulation of this universal principle in the realm of inner vision: the *Sambhogakaya,* the "Body of Bliss" (rapture or spiritual enjoyment), from which all true inspiration is born; (3) that, in which this inspiration is transformed into visible form and becomes action: the *Nirmanakaya:* the 'Body of Transformation', the human embodiment or individuality of an Enlightened One."[64]

So, the Father, or the Dharmakaya, is the embodiment of all the known, all laws, all forms or experiences, all existence. Out of this body comes the Son or the Sambhogakaya. One of the attributes of Sambhogakaya is play, which has the quality of mischievousness, and also it has the quality of a sense of humor, an uplifting light-hearted quality, which is beyond ego's heavy-handed nature. This humor seems to be associated with a sense of futility, but at the level of celebrating one's life.

The path to the Sambhogakaya may not come gently, but rather as an "accident" or a "catastrophe," or a "disaster." Perhaps the experience of the Sambhogakaya can be likened to a scene in Kazantzakis' book *Zorba the Greek.* Toward the end, when the lumber was being slid down the cables, the narrator says, "Impossible to describe what happened then. The catastrophe burst upon us like a thunderbolt. We had scarcely time to run away. The entire structure swayed. The pine tree, which the workmen had attached to the cable, assumed a demonic impetus. Sparks flew, large splinters of wood shot through the air, and when the tree arrived at the bottom a few seconds later it was no more than a charred log."[65] After such a catastrophe, there was nothing left to do but eat, drink, learn to dance and go on with one's life. Later, in a conversation we find, "'I say boss,' he said, 'did you see the showers of sparks the thing threw out?' We burst out laughing. Zorba threw himself on me, embraced and kissed me. 'Does it make you laugh, too?' he said tenderly. 'Are you laughing, too? Eh, boss? Good!' Rocking with laughter we wrestled playfully with one another for some time."[66]

Perhaps another example in literature are the writings of Flannery O'Connor. She is considered one of the foremost short-story writers in American Literature. An anomaly among post-World War II authors – a Roman Catholic from the Bible-belt **South whose stated purpose was to reveal the mystery of God's grace in everyday life.** Her short-stories lead to most unpleasant and sometimes disastrous endings, leaving the reader in a most uncomfortable state.

The Sambhogakaya is transmitted into the Nirmanakaya (Holy Spirit) which is our present situation, that state of existence which is an Earthly, physical, bodily situation, because everything that we experience becomes the visual and audio world in the ordinary sense, where the sun rises and sets, the tide ebbs and flows, and the moon wanes and waxes. Somehow, however, we do not quite see it in its complete Holy Spirit or Nirmanakaya aspect. To experience the Trikaya or Holy Trinity is what one seeks spiritually.

Iconography

Iconography comes from the Greek word "icon" meaning image, and "graphy" meaning to write. So iconography literally means "image writing." The word has come to usually indicate a sacred image, though it really means much more than that. The subject of iconography can be some spiritual person or some spiritual event from spiritual history, or a symbol such as a mandala (which contains the 5 elements, as previously discussed). Iconography is the art of expressing the spiritual reality of these people and events using sacred symbolic forms and mystical colors. The drawings are made with precision, drawn more like a mechanical drawing than art. Yet, through iconography deeper realities can be presented in an objective way, and can open up new worlds to the practitioner as well as to those who meditate upon them. Iconography is the visual relationship to the divine. It is rich with visual correspondences.

Mantras

If I had to define poetry, I would define it as the ability to produce vivid images with a few well-chosen words. In that sense, Mantras are the epitome of poetry, having the potential to create the image of an entire realm with a few simple sounds.

Mantras are the utilization of a sound or series of syllables to connect with their deep correspondence. They are frequently utilized during true rituals along with corresponding mudras (hand gestures) and images. There are literally thousands of mantras. One of the best known is the mantra "OM MANI PADME HUM," which in China is Quan Yin's mantra, and in Tibet, the mantra of Avalokiteshvara. OM symbolizes "the origin, the Supreme Source, the Dharmakaya, the Absolute."[67] MANI PADME signifies "such pairs of concepts as: the essential wisdom lying at the heart of Buddhist doctrine; ... Mind contained within our minds; the eternal within the temporal; ... the goal (supreme wisdom) and the means (compassion)."[68]

HUM corresponds to "the conditioned in the unconditioned; ... it represents limitless."[69]

But a mantra does not produce its full correspondence with the deepest levels of one's consciousness if one's mind is cluttered with verbal concepts. Reflective thought must be transcended, abandoned to experience the correspondence.

The Mozart Effect – Positive Influence of Music and the Arts

The positive effects of Mozart's music has come to the public's attention largely through Don Campbell's book *The Mozart Effect: Tapping the Power of Music to Heal the Body, Strengthen the Mind and Unlock the Creative Spirit.* Here are just a few of the hundreds of reported benefits obtained from listening to Mozart: (1) improving test scores (2) cutting learning time, (3) calming hyperactive children and adults, (4) reducing errors, (5) improving creativity and clarity, (6) healing the body faster, (7) integrating both sides of the brain for more efficient learning, (8) raising IQ scores 9 points on the average (research done at University of California, Irvine). It might also surprise our scientific community to know that, (1) in a study of medical school applicants, 66% of music majors who applied to medical school were admitted, the highest percentage of any group, compared with only 44% of biochemistry majors; (2) the very best engineers and technical designers in the Silicon Valley industry are, nearly without exception, practicing musicians; (3) students who study music scored higher on both the verbal and math portions of the SAT than non-music students. Engaging individuals in the visual arts have obtained similar results.

The knowledge of the impact of music and the arts on humankind is surprisingly old. Grof notes, "In many cultures, sound technology has been used specifically for healing purposes in the context of intricate ceremonies. The Navajo healing rituals conducted by trained singers have astounding complexity that has been compared to that of the scripts of Wagnerian operas. The trance dance of the Kung Bushmen in the African Kalahari Desert has enormous healing power, as has been documented in several anthropological studies and movies."[70] Don Campbell tells us that "for nearly a decade I lived in Haiti and Japan where my traditional training [as a musician] was greatly expanded. I saw the drumming, singing and dancing of Haiti induce states of deep trance and transformation. I saw hundreds of people enter into altered states of consciousness. Sometimes bleeding would cease, physical diseases would instantly heal and endless psychological dilemmas would balance."[71]

We find in Waldorf education a similar understanding of the value of art and music. Rudolf Steiner developed Waldorf education in Europe in the 1920s, basing this educational system on his understanding of subtle bodies. He believed that we understood the etheric body through the sculptural process, understanding how curves and shapes grow out of inner forces. The astral body, in turn, is connected with music.

The aim of Waldorf education is to educate the whole child – head, heart and hands. The curriculum is geared to the child's stages of development and brings together all elements – intellectual, artistic, spiritual and movement. The goal is to enable individuals, in and of themselves, to impart meaning to their lives and to realize their interconnectedness with all of life.

As M.C. Richards puts it, "Why does the human being long to work artistically? Why are the art programs ... so popular? Because there is a natural enthusiasm for creativity built into our bodies. There is an essential connection between artistic activity and human nature, between art and nature and universe and human being. Painting, modeling, music, movement, speech, architecture, and drama are not electives. They are the ground of our intuitive understanding of ourselves and the world around us."[72] Barbara Kazanis reminds us that the role of art is to make the invisible visible, to provide the language of expression for the ineffable. When the artist creates out of authentic primary sources, the intersection between voice, movement, image and word become an eloquent language that contains and expresses life energy. In this view our lived life is recognized to be the source of our formalized or ritualized works. Art arises from clear perception of our sense, emotions, and thoughts, and the arts are basic because they arise from and reveal to us a fundamental quality of mind that is not accessible any other way.[73]

One would have to say that the transforming effect of music and art is regarded as natural in most cultures. Music, the arts, Waldorf Education, can be seen as the effects of the science of correspondence, thinking metaphorically, experiencing the world metaphorically, and connecting with our deeper selves.

Superstition

The etymology of superstition is from the Latin for standing over. Superstition is really the remnants of a higher level of thinking involved in the science of correspondence. To distinguish between how we see superstition today and authentic metaphorical thinking requires substantial studying (just as does our logic). Indeed, if one is not skilled in metaphorical thinking, one will make incorrect associations which lead to superstition, just as poor logic can lead to incorrect conclusions. One must immerse oneself in this process, be open but critical, questioning, to pursue his type of process appropriately. If one is truly knowledgeable of the correspondences, it is easy to distinguish superstition from correspondence, and superstition, then, is not an issue.

When it comes to other peoples beliefs, be it so called primitive cultures or ancient cultures, the Western world with its scientific perspective regards those views often as superstitious, and seldom suspects that there is anything of significance (particularly of scientific significance) that these cultures have to teach us. The tendency has been to disregard all science of correspondence concepts as superstitious. The West has made it clear to other cultures that they should suppress their beliefs or understandings of the universe in our presence, and they obligingly do so. As a result, we miss out on some valuable concepts, knowledge, and wisdom. We always (and naturally so) try to analyze their lives in terms of <u>our</u> present understandings of the universe, i.e. in terms of what we presently "know." To do so is to ignore the great potential for mystery, which could expand our present, limited understandings. To understand the beliefs of other cultures we must suspend our own doubts and ignorance and open to their world, not intellectually, by taking notes and physical measurements, but experientially – becoming a part of their world. To understand the third world, one must live in it, opened minded, for a considerable length of time just to scratch the surface. Few of us have time to do so, and those topics associated with the science of correspondence will appear like superstition to the logically trained Western mind.

LIMITATIONS OF WESTERN SCIENCE

"The determination of scientists not to ask questions that cannot be answered empirically, and proved logically, has led to a drastic shrinkage of philosophical territory: philosophy is now identified with logic, deductive and inductive, and it is the claim of the scientific philosophers that no other mental activity deserves the name of philosophy. Logical formulas have taken the place of what the scientist calls 'the picture language of speculative systems', and on a diet of such dry dog biscuits modern man is asked to undertake his spiritual Odyssey." – Herbert Read, The Forms of Things Unknown

Scientists tend to believe that they know the limits on what is possible, but actually they know the minimal that is possible, for one never knows what breakthrough in science will expand the limits on what is possible. Science has both methodological limitations inherent in its system, and political limitations placed on the science by many in the scientific community. Most people who operate outside of the scientific community do not understand the strong resistance that mainstream science offers to psychic/spiritual phenomena. It is difficult to explain where this resistance comes from, and yet one feels compelled to address this issue in order to understand why so little is done to explore the spiritual/psychic phenomena mentioned in this book. In fact, most of the phenomena mentioned in this book are off the radar screen of the mainstream scientific community. As mentioned, much of this appears like superstition to these scientists, who truly believe that they are saving the world from superstition. So here we attempt to show where this resistance comes from and why so little experimentation is performed in the exploration of these phenomena.

Due to specialization, today's scientists are trained in a very limited perspective of knowledge. Very few have the opportunity to even explore other sciences in any depth, let alone subjects like the philosophy of science. Mainstream scientists tend to feel they understand how science operates, and as a result they do not know what they don't know. Their perspective paints a picture of the universe in which they find security, but philosophers and poets may not. The vast majority of scientists are "mainstream" or "hard-core" scientists. They perform traditional scientific tasks and do not explore that which violates the presently accepted paradigm of science. To these scientists the existing paradigm dictates what is possible and what is not possible. This had led to the adage that scientists can't see beyond the end of their "knows."

The "visionary" scientists are people like Newton, Schrödinger, Einstein, Pauli, Heisenberg, De Broglie, Hawking, Jung, and many others. The "visionary" scientist has a better understanding of the capabilities and limits of science, whereas the mainstream scientist is a "true believer" of science and often does not understand the limitations of science. Mainstream scientists have been taught to distrust experience, which is regarded as misleading. It is interesting to contrast this with the artist who views the variations and inconsistencies in human experience as what are of interest to explore. To the scientist the lack of reproducibility from person to person, (or these "misconceptions"), are the problems which need to be avoided in order to perform controlled, objective experiments.

Experience is distrusted in science because it seemingly has led to incorrect conclusions. The classical example is the perception of falling objects. Before Galileo, it was assumed that heavy objects fall faster than light objects. Clearly a feather falls more slowly than a rock. But beneath that "superficial" observation was a powerful secret. Galileo performed careful experiments using an inclined plane (to slow down the falling movement), and a water clock to measure the time of this motion. He discovered that for objects rolling down the inclined plane at a given slope or angle, their motion was essentially independent of their weight. Furthermore he discovered that the distance traveled was proportional to the time squared, and not to the time. In other words, the object was accelerating uniformly. The concept of acceleration becomes important in developing Newton's Laws of Motion. Galileo would eventually climb to the top of the Leaning Tower of Pisa and simultaneously drop two objects of significant weight difference, and they hit the ground at the same time. Prior to Galileo one might have suspected that an object of twice the weight of another object might reach the ground in half the time. Without this careful experimentation and measurement, our understanding of the behavior of falling objects was inaccurate. These simple experiments opened the door to Newton's Laws of Motion.

The scientist can point to countless situations where man's beliefs where incorrect prior to scientific exploration. This has led many scientists to simply state that we cannot trust our intuitions, or our experiences.

But there are also countless situations of the following. We should recall that in 1903, a soon to be Nobel Prize Laureate, Albert Abraham Michelson, stated that "The more important fundamental laws and facts of physical science have all been discovered, and these are now so firmly established that the possibility of their ever being supplanted in consequence of new discoveries is exceedingly remote."[74]

And another well-known physicist (Lord Kelvin) stated over 100 years ago that the job of physics was essentially complete and students should not bother to pursue a career in Physics. Both these statements are of course, before quantum mechanics, before relativity, before high-energy and nuclear physics, before elementary particles, before chaos theory, etc.

Scientific perceptions are often incorrect. One hundred years ago, the entire universe was thought to lie in the Milky Way and there was no big bang concept, but rather a steady state universe which had no beginning or end. One hundred years ago, even though the nuclear power of the sun was literally staring them in the face, scientists didn't see it as nuclear energy, but as thermal energy generated by the gravitational contraction of the sun. One hundred years ago scientists believed they had explained all physical phenomena in terms of the laws of physics available to them. It is not unusual to make things fit in terms of our understandings, and if that doesn't work, often the phenomena is ignored or disbelieved.

Even today mainstream scientists really don't anticipate any major changes in their perspective of the universe or of the present paradigm. They never do. Their effort is more aimed at either ignoring what they can't explain, or trying to make the observation fit the model, just as Lord Kelvin made the energy of the sun fit into thermal energy. An example of that today might be Dr. Francis Crick, Nobel Prize Laureate, who has recently published a book entitled *The Astonishing Hypothesis,* about which he suggests that "everything that you see and feel, your emotions, and so on, all that, on this hypothesis is due to the activities of nerve cells and other molecular events going on inside your brain, and it is not necessary to postulate something external ... that you might call the soul. ... His book sketches the science of just one kind of consciousness, the visual, but in all that we perceive, interpret and remember, everything that we've identified with mind and spirit, all of it, he says, is just the firing of tiny electrical charges in the neuron of the brain. He says his campaign is to engage scientists in the study of consciousness, to appropriate the well worked turf of philosophers and theologians, and explore it with the tools of experimental science."[75] Yet he admits that he cannot provide conclusive evidence for what he wants to believe. Clearly Dr. Francis Crick does not anticipate any significant new discoveries.

If we follow the history and philosophy of science as Thomas S. Kuhn did in *The Structure of Scientific Revolutions,* we find that transitions in paradigms (universally recognized scientific achievements that for a time provide model problems and solutions to a community of practitioners) undergo significant upheavals and are not as smooth or as clear cut or as logical as we are led to believe in retrospect.[76]

Schrödinger, a great scientist himself, whose wave equation became the foundation of quantum mechanics, understood the limits of science quite well. In his book, *My View of the World,* he states:

"The scientific picture of the real world around me is very deficient. It gives a lot of factual information, puts all our experience in a magnificently consistent order, but it is ghastly silent about all and sundry that is really near to our heart, that really matters to us. It cannot tell us a word about red and blue, bitter and sweet, physical pain and physical delight; it knows nothing of beautiful and ugly, good or bad, God and eternity. Science sometimes pretends to answer questions in these domains, but the answers are very often so silly that we are not inclined to take them seriously.

"So in brief, we do not belong to this material world that science constructs for us. We are not in it; we are outside. We are only spectators. The reason why we believe that we are in it, that we belong to the picture, is that our bodies are in the picture. Our bodies belong to it. Not only my own body, but those of my friends, also of my dog and cat and horse, and of all the other people and animals. And this is my only means of communicating with them."[77]

Schrödinger goes on to say:

"The scientific world-picture vouchsafes a very complete understanding of all that happens – it makes it just a little too understandable. It allows you to imagine the total display as that of a mechanical clockwork which, for all that science knows, could go on just the same as it does, without there being consciousness, will, endeavor, pain and delight and responsibility connected with it – though they actually are. And the reason for this disconcerting situation is just this: that for the purpose of constructing the picture of the external world, we have used the greatly simplifying device of cutting our own personality out, removing it; hence it is gone, it has evaporated, it is ostensibly not needed.

"In particular, and most importantly, this is the reason why the scientific worldview contains of itself no ethical values, no esthetical values, not a word about our own ultimate scope or destination, and no God, if you please. Whence came I and whither go I?"[78]

Schrödinger makes it clear that present day science cannot answer, or even approach the basic questions we have about the universe, such as who we are, why we are here, and how we should live. Is there a God? a soul? etc. Many other scientists and non-scientists alike have over the years, made similar observation about science. In the 20th century science has been so silent on these questions – unable to even approach them – that mainstream scientists have tacitly concluded that these questions are not worth pursuing, and are of no value.

Schrödinger is not ridiculing science. In fact he has a high regard for his profession. He is simply stating what should be an obvious truth about the limits of science as it is practiced today. If science is to begin to move beyond these limitations, its basic premise must be expanded. Science is presently locked into logic as the only way that meaningful connections can occur and conclusions can be made. Scientists hide behind their "objectivity" to nullify any direct experiential knowledge.

Despite the incredible successes of Western science, it nevertheless has been unable to answer one significant spiritual issue. Carl Sagan has said that what he likes about science is that you if you have a question, you can determine a scientific test for this question, perform the experiment and gather the data and reach a conclusion. This "statement" has the illusion of truth because scientists limit their thinking to those situations where this is true. However, significant spiritual issues do not lend themselves so easily to this type of logical process. In an obvious sense, God not being definable cannot be put to a scientific test. But we also find that spiritual issues often lead to a win-win situation. For example the goddess Quan Yin, who if you pray to her for something and she does not grant your prayer, it is accepted that she has a very good reason, and one accepts that. Such a win-win situation makes it impossible to put such concepts to a logical test. The scientist might conclude one is only deluding oneself to believe such a thing, but there is no scientific proof for that conclusion either.

Spiritual enlightenment is regarded as the goal of the spiritual path, and although one might look upon enlightenment as an answer, it could equally be viewed as a question, since it is beyond duality. Being so, it does not lend itself to logical scientific exploration.

Godel's discovery of the limitations of logic also places limits on scientific investigation. A century ago it was believed that given a sufficient set of premises, a statement could be logically proved or disproved. However, Godel has shown that this is not true of logic – not all consequences of a fundamental set of theorems can be proved, even though the consequence may be consistent with the theorems. Not all questions can be answered logically.

Another limitation of science comes from Heisenberg and the Uncertainty Principle, which limits our precision of logical knowledge, and points out that to make a measurement, one interferes with or affects the system one is measuring.

More recently, chaos theory has shown us that the solutions of certain types of mathematical equations (such as second order non-linear differential equations) cannot be written as a traditional equation. These types of equations cannot be solved by clever mathematical tricks, but require a computer to describe the solutions. Furthermore, the path of the solution is unpredictable. All of this came as a great surprise to mathematicians and scientists alike. As long as science chose to ignore these equations (and scientists did so because they couldn't solve them), the universe looked logically predictable. Now it does not appear so.

Transpersonal experiences in general do not lend themselves to scientific scrutiny. As Stanislav Grof states: "Transpersonal experiences have many strange characteristics that shatter the most fundamental assumptions of materialistic science and of the mechanistic worldview. Researchers who have seriously studied and/or experienced these fascinating phenomena realize that the attempts of traditional psychiatry to dismiss them as irrelevant products of imagination or as erratic fantasmagoria generated by pathological processes in the brain are superficial and inadequate. Any unbiased study of the transpersonal domain of the psyche has to come to the conclusion that the observations involved represent a critical challenge for the Newtonian-Cartesian paradigm of Western science."[79]

To better explore transpersonal experiences, we need to understand the nature of humankind's total consciousness. What we normally regard as the unconscious can become conscious as we shift our consciousness to subtle bodies. From the etheric body, the visible body and etheric body are conscious and the astral body, mental body, etc. are still unconscious. As we shift our consciousness deeper and deeper, more activities of the subtle bodies become conscious. Techniques for experiencing the subtle bodies and the unconscious are best explained by Swedenborg's "science of correspondence."

CONCLUSION

"The most beautiful thing we can experience is the mysterious. It is the source of all true art and science. He to whom this emotion is a stranger, who no longer pauses to wonder and stand in rapt awe, is as good as dead." – Albert Einstein

The physical basis of mysticism was presented in Chapters I and II. These Chapters showed how mystics have viewed the physical world, how consistent this view is with modern science, and how this view provides a logical explanation for psychic/spiritual/transpersonal phenomena. The present Chapter shows how the experience of mystical phenomena can be accomplished through a metaphorical science, the science of correspondence. The utilization of metaphorical thinking and processes has the ability to open the doors to other realms of existence, here-to-fore doubted by Western science.

How can the events discussed in this book be accounted for by physicists, chemists, or by biologists? Although science has been unable to account for such phenomena, there is no reason for doubting that they can be scientifically accounted for. This book provides such a physical basis. We have outlined how science can be expanded to include subtle matter, subtle bodies and subtle energy. This subtle matter is, in essence, the heart of what science today calls dark matter. Essentially, the problem for scientists is that the scientific laws they utilize are limited to visible matter, and they may need to enter into the realm of actually experiencing this subtle matter and subtle bodies before they can grasp the physical laws related to subtle matter and the anatomical laws related to the subtle bodies with their nadis and chakras. "Scientists today believe that people are composed of matter created by the Big Bang and then processed in the stars into the atoms of the elements. This is true for our visible body, but in addition to this body, a much older tradition says that we also have subtle bodies composed of matters created at different stages in the development of the universe, which predate the Big Bang."[80] We need to look within us with our sophisticated instruments, or perhaps our subtle vision, to prove to ourselves that we too, as well as the galactic halos, consist of dark matter. It is not outside of our present scientific abilities to do so, if we choose to put our creative powers into this exploration.

Over the past 100 years, science has gone from a macroscopic view of matter to an atomic view of matter, to the subatomic view of matter and what is presently believed to be its most basic building blocks (quarks, electrons, neutrinos). Science has also gone from a steady state universe containing one galaxy (the milky way), to a Big Bang theory dating the Universe at about 15 to 20 billion years and containing about 50 billion galaxies. We have made great strides in directions undreamed of 100 years ago, in all fields of science. We have gone to the moon and reached out to the planets. The next great direction for man to explore will certainly be subtle matter, subtle bodies, and the dimensions it leads us into, the spiritual dimension of humankind and its multifaceted components. Other cultures have gone before us with this knowledge, but we can systematically explore these dimensions, perhaps as no culture has before. Certainly an exploration of this type will prove to be of greater value than even the previous 100 years of phenomenal scientific accomplishments, and attract the most creative amongst us. How can we resist exploring man's spirituality?

John Mbiti states that in Africa, "the spiritual universe is a unit with the physical, and that these two intermingle and dovetail into each other so much that it is not easy, or even necessary, at times to draw the distinction or separate them."[81] Experiences of the subtle bodies and the world they relate to are what we encounter when we have spiritual experiences. These worlds are beyond our daily experiences, and so they are very difficult to explain – we have no vocabulary to discuss or explore them in the West. It is like trying to describe the color "red" to a person who has never seen the color "red." We might start by explaining that it is not yellow, it is not blue, it is not green, it is not white, it is not black, etc. This may lead the person to believe that you must be referring to a very negative state of color, not having any of the usual colors in it. This is the conclusion often drawn by Westerners when reading about eastern spirituality – they conclude, because of all the negation referred to in describing these states of mind, that one is talking about states of mind void of anything worthwhile. But that's obviously not the case.

We live in the most intellectual culture that the world has ever known. Yet our religions offer very little in the way of intellectual appeal, unable to successfully bridge this gap. Too often those who claim to represent spirituality in fact do not. This all too frequently turns people away from any consideration of the spiritual path, and leads many to believe that religion has nothing to offer. The techniques utilized by the science of correspondence offer considerable intellectual stimulation, and, if successful, eventually leads to a personal experiential understanding of spirituality. Ultimately, the transformation process which allows consciousness on the level of the spirit (the sambhogakaya, the ananda-maya-kosa) is the process of the spiritual path.

Today in the Western world and elsewhere, one is told to have faith, and not to question. Ultimately, at some juncture, one may require a leap of faith, but that leap comes after years of pursuing and questioning, riding oneself of reasonable doubts. True spirituality requires questioning as does true science. One should not be deluded into believing one "believes" when one

138

does not and one still has many unanswered questions. Too often our "religious teachers" cannot answer our questions because they have not had a spiritual awakening themselves and therefore discourage the asking of questions, telling one to have faith. This truly discourages a scientific mind, and can encourage a fanaticism, and fanaticism is not religion, is not spirituality. As Stanislav Grof notes, "The spirituality that emerges spontaneously at a certain stage of experiential self-exploration should not be confused with the mainstream religions and their beliefs, doctrines, dogmas, and rituals. Many of them lost entirely the connection with their original source, which is a direct visionary experience of transpersonal realities. They are mainly concerned with such issues as power, money, hierarchies, and ethical, political, and social control. It is possible to have a religion with very little spirituality, complete absence thereof, or even one that interferes with genuine spiritual quest." [82]

From a physical point of view, the spiritual path can be seen as the experience of or consciousness of the subtle bodies. We live in several realms of existence simultaneously. Spirituality through the subtle bodies, opens the door to direct experiences of near-death experiences, out-of-body experiences, death-rebirth sequences, past incarnation memories, psychic experiences, sides (special powers), spontaneous experiences of the mystic light, encounters with archetypal entities, transpersonal visions, feelings of cosmic consciousness, and universal love. It is on this level that the shaman finds the entire world to be alive, to be enchanted.

The subtle body doctrine of mysticism has passed the test of time, being a part of our ancient to modern cultures, throughout the world. It provides an excellent foundation for the explanation of numerous phenomena (as included in this book) so that even without a physical basis it is a valuable system well worth exploring and utilizing. Its success in mystical traditions and the scientific verification of much of the phenomena mentioned here are sufficient to warrant subtle body theory as a valuable doctrine. Truly, it needs no further proof. However, the way in which mystics describe subtle matter is consistent with the properties of recently discovered "dark matter," and so this possibility for a connection with Western science is quite real and could be of great significant benefit. This seems to verify that we have a soul, and it is physical, even though it is a very fine form of physical dark matter. But we must be aware that the *intellectual* understanding of this doctrine will not enlighten mankind; we must obtain an *experiential* awareness of the subtle bodies in order to truly benefit from these teachings. We need to better grasp the generalized view of what science is, to include the science of correspondence. In so doing, we will be able to live our lives from a deeper sympathetic understanding of the nature of man and of our position in the universe. We will better understand the consequences of our actions and decisions, on a personal level, a social level, a global level, and a universal level.

As we explore the teachings of mysticism, we will find that different cultures explain these concepts differently. The reason is that each culture being unique relates to and values different aspects of mysticism and the subtle bodies. For example, in our culture, different disciplines relate to the same object in different ways. If we look at an apple, the physicist would be interested in its mass and density; the chemist in its chemical composition; the artist is its shape, form and color; the chef in its taste and texture; the economist in its market value; the lawyer in ownership; the theologian in its role in the Garden of Eden; and so on. If you didn't know what an apple was, you could regard all these viewpoints as contradictory and conclude that they all can't be right. Similarly different cultures have discussed the subtle bodies and chakras differently because of their different values and interests. This is not a weakness in subtle body and chakra theory, but indicates independent discovery and development by each culture. Western science with its unequaled detail and precision will certainly have to find its own conceptual language in order to discuss these properties of subtle "dark matter," subtle bodies and chakras.

Our world should not be limited to the truths science holds *at present*. It seems all too natural to do so if we think science contains absolute truths, and science seems to be capable of so much. But science contains relative truths and is not capable of satisfying our deeper needs. Science cannot tell us who we are and why we are here, and without that knowledge we cannot understand how to best live our lives or utilize our modern technology. It is difficult to see the holes or limitations of our present scientific theories, but clearly if one wishes to believe in science in some absolute way, one has to ask, which science are you speaking of – the science of 200 years ago when we knew all about Newton's Laws but believed that electricity and magnetism were independent phenomena; or the science of 100 years ago which knew that electricity and magnetism and light were all properties of electrical charge but still did not know of quantum mechanics, or nuclear physics, or high-energy physics, or elementary particles, or special relativity, etc.; or do we speak of the science of today when we "obviously" have all the major truths; or perhaps the science of 100 years from now, or the science of 200 years from now, and who would dare to guess which scientific truths will hold up to their present status 1000 years from now. But looking back only 100 years makes one realize that, although scientists believed that they understood all the major scientific truths in physics, they could not see what they didn't know, and in reality, they had only begun. Today we are in the same situation. Sometimes we think that when we describe something we understand why it is so, but description is not explanation. We do not know why there are physical laws even though we can understand and utilize them in great detail; and even though we can describe the events immediately after the big bang, we do not know how this uncaused event could have occurred, or if it could happen again. As Stephen Hawking states "a scientific theory is just a mathematical model we make to describe our observations: it exists only in our minds."[83]

In our own physical body, we do not know how we are able with our mind to redirect the cause-effect phenomena and move our bodies, speak our thoughts, seemingly at will, thus producing an uncaused effect. This ability to do so must come from "outside" our "visible" bodies. In his book *What is Life,* Schrödinger states: "(i) My body functions as a pure mechanism according to the Laws of Nature. (ii) Yet I know, by incontrovertible direct experience, that I am directing its motions, of which I foresee the effects, that may be fateful and all-important, in which I feel and take full responsibility for them. ... The only possible inference from these two facts is, I think, that I – I in the widest meaning of the word, that is to say, every conscious mind that has ever said or felt 'I' – am the person, if any, who controls the 'motion of the atoms' according to the Laws of Nature"[84]

To put it another way, the ability to utilize and direct the cause and effect laws of nature so that one can control the motion of one's body within these laws of nature, must come from a source outside those laws of physics associated with the visible body.

Science seems to be in a perpetual state of believing it has the truth, despite its history of changing paradigms. This failure to accept the idea of "mysterium" is surprising, because there will always be a great mystery out there waiting to be discovered. The Universe is not so small, nor so unimaginative as to lend itself to total analysis by a logical science. This does not diminish the value of science, but simply places it in an appropriate perspective. Science provides one type of insight into the workings of the universe, but not the only insight. The arts certainly provide another route to knowledge, and mysticism provides yet another. The combination of logical science (Western science) and analogical science (science of correspondence) can help us to understand our role in the universe, and to appreciate the universe as the extraordinary multifaceted phenomena it truly is.

Chapter 5

Personal Accounts

INTRODUCTION

The spectrum of the human experience seems limitless. People from all walks of life have had experiences which are beyond our normal limited understanding of the universe. There are countless examples. Usually these experiences have a profound impact on the individual. The following are just a few representational stories, in an effort to demonstrate several different types of encounters that people have. These stories suggest the existence of subtle bodies and the transcendent nature of humankind.

1. Reincarnation

Most cultures accept reincarnation as fact, and we in the West are discovering that children often remember their past lives. Dr. Ian Stevenson has documented numerous accounts of past lives, using stringent scientific criteria. The following is a well documented story of apparent reincarnation. Notice the skepticism of her parents, even though they live in a culture which accepts reincarnation in theory.

Told by Frank Edwards, from *Stranger Than Science Fiction*, New York, NY: Lyle Stuart , Inc.

The parents of Shanti Devi lived quietly in Delhi, India, where she was born in 1926. There was nothing unusual about her birth – nothing at all that might have warned her parents of what was to follow.

144

As the little girl began to grow out of her babyhood, her mother noticed that she often seemed confused. She kept to herself and sometimes seemed to be talking to an imaginary person.

It was not until she was seven years old, however, that her parents became worried about her sanity. That was the year that little Shanti told her mother that she had lived before, in a town called Muttra. She even described the house where she claimed to have lived in this earlier life.

Her mother told Shanti's father. He, in turn, took the child to a doctor, who questioned her closely. After the child had told her strange story, the doctor could explain nothing. If the little girl was ill, it was a most unusual illness. And if not, then he dared not guess at the truth. He told the father to question the child from time to time and to write down the answers.

Shanti Devi never changed her story. By the time she was nine years old her parents were not surprised at anything she told them. In truth, they had come to believe that something was definitely wrong with her mind. It was in 1935 that the girl told her parents that she had given birth to three children. She described the youngsters and gave their names. She claimed that her own name in that first life had been Ludgi.

Her parents only smiled and tried to hide their sadness.

One evening while Shanti and her mother were preparing the evening meal, there was a knock at the door. The girl ran to open it. When she failed to return soon, her mother began to wonder what was keeping her. She found Shanti staring at a strange man who stood at the steps. The child said, "Mother! This is the cousin of my husband!"

The stranger did live in Muttra! He had come to talk business with Shanti's father. He did not recognize Shanti. But he told her parents that he had a cousin whose wife, named Ludgi, had died in childbirth ten years before. The worried parents told him of their daughter's strange story about a former life. He agreed to get his cousin to come to Delhi to see if Shanti could recognize him.

The girl was told nothing of the plan. But when the strange man arrived, she threw herself in his arms and sobbed that he was her husband ... come back to her. The confused man went with Shanti's parents to the local government office, where they told their amazing story. The government of India appointed a special committee of scientists to check into the case.

Had the dead woman, Ludgi, really come back to life in the body of Shanti Devi?

The scientists took Shanti to the town of Muttra. As she stepped off the train, she pointed out and correctly named the mother and brother of the man she said had been her husband. Soon she was talking to them in the Indian dialect used in Muttra, although the dialect she had learned from her parents was quite different.

The puzzled scientists continued their test. They blindfolded the girl and put her into a carriage, climbing in beside her. She directed the driver through the town, described the different places they passed – and finally ordered him to stop at the end of a narrow street. "This," she said, "is where I lived!" When the bandages were removed from her eyes, she saw an old man who sat smoking in front of the house. "That man was my father-in-law," she told them. And, indeed, he had been the father-in-law of Ludgi!

Oddly, she recognized the two oldest children; but not the youngest, whose birth had cost Ludgi's life.

The scientists were careful in their comments. They agreed that somehow the child born in Delhi seemed to remember a life in Muttra, and to remember it in amazing detail. The scientists reported that they could find nothing that suggested a trick. Neither could they find an explanation for what they had seen.

The full story of Shanti Devi, now living quietly as a government worker in New Delhi, can be found in medical and government reports. In 1958 she told doctors who questioned her that she had learned to live in the present; that the old yearning for her past no longer bothered her.

2. The Rainbow Body

The rainbow body is believed to manifest in those who have attained a very high level of spiritual awareness. It is said that if one achieves the rainbow body, then at death the dense, visible body will transform into the wisdom body, and no remnant of the visible body will be found except for fingernails and some hair. The following is a recent documentation of such an event.

Told by Sogyal Rinpoche, from *The Tibetan Book of Living and Dying,* New York NY: HarperSanFrancisco. 1992, p. 167-169.

Through these advanced practices of Dzogchen, accomplished practitioners can bring their lives to an extraordinary and triumphant end. As they die, they enable their body to be reabsorbed back into the light essence of the elements that created it, and consequently their material body dissolves into light and then disappears completely. This process is known as the "rainbow body" or "body of light," because the dissolution is often accomplished by spontaneous manifestations of light and rainbows. The ancient Tantras of Dzogchen, and the writings of the great masters, distinguish different categories of this amazing, otherworldly phenomenon, for at one time, if at least not normal, it was reasonably frequent.

Usually a person who knows he or she is about to attain the rainbow body will ask to be left alone and undisturbed in a room or a tent for seven days. On the eighth day only the hair and nails, the impurities of the body, are found.

This may be very difficult for us now to believe, but the factual history of the Dzogchen lineage is full of examples of individuals who attained the rainbow body, and as Dudjom Rinpoche often used to point out, this is not just ancient history. Of the many examples I would like to choose one of the most recent, and one with which I have a personal connection. In 1952 there was a famous instance of the rainbow body in the east of Tibet, witnessed by many people. The man who attained it, Sonam Mangyal, was the father of my tutor and the brother of Lama Tseten. ...

He was a very simple, humble person, who made his way as an itinerant stone carver, carving mantras and sacred texts. Some say he had been a hunter in his youth, and had received teaching from a great master. No one really knew he was a practitioner; he was truly what is called "a hidden yogin." Some time before his death, he would be seen to go up into the mountains and just sit, silhouette against the skyline, gazing up into space. He composed his own songs and chants and sung them instead of the traditional ones. No one had any idea what he was doing. He then fell ill, or seemed to, but became, strangely, increasingly happy. When the illness got worse, his family called in masters and doctors. His son told him he should remember all the teachings he had heard, and he smiled and said, "I've forgotten them all and anyway, there's nothing to remember. Everything is illusion, but I am confident that all is well."

Just before his death at seventy-nine, he said: "All I ask is that when I die, don't move my body for a week." When he died his family wrapped his body and invited Lamas and monks to come and practice for him. They placed the body in a small room in the house, and they could not help noticing that although he had been a tall person, they had no trouble getting it in, as if he were becoming smaller. At the same time, an extraordinary display of rainbow-colored light was seen all around the house. When they looked into the room on the sixth day, they saw that the body was getting smaller and smaller. On the eighth day after his death, the morning on which the funeral had been arranged, the undertakers arrived to collect his body. When they undid its coverings, they found nothing inside but his nails and hair.

My master Jamyang Khyentse asked for these to be brought to him, and verified that this was a case of the rainbow body.

3. Kundalini Experience

The following is a well-written account of the Kundalini experience, a special energy that is processed through the central channel and the charkas of the subtle bodies.

Anonymously told, from *The Adventure of Self-Discovery*, by Stanislav Grof, Albany, NY: State University of New York Press. 1988, p. 115-116

As I continued to breathe, I started feeling an incredible upsurge of energy in my pelvis. In my sacral area was a powerful source of light and heat that was radiating in all directions. And then this energy started to stream upward along my spinal cord, following a clearly defined line. On the way, it was lighting up additional sources of energy in the places where the esoteric maps place the different charkas.

As this was happening, I was experiencing very blissful orgiastic feelings. One of the most powerful experiences of this session was when this energy reached the area of my heart. I felt such incredible love toward the world and toward other people that I wanted to get up and give a big hug to everybody in the group. It was strange how close I felt toward other people whom I had met last night for the first time and whom I did not really know.

But I stayed with the experience and the energy continued to flow upward. When it reached the top of my head, it exploded into a fantastically beautiful aureole that had a rosy-orange hue, like the pictures of the Thousand Petal Lotus. I felt the need to flex my legs and join the soles of my feet to create a closed circuit of energy. My energetic field was now extended far beyond the boundaries of my physical body; I suddenly understood why the esoteric maps show the subtle energy body as much larger than the mental body; one can actually experience it that way in these states.

The energy was flowing upward, leaving through the top of my head and then returning to the lower parts of my body to participate again in the upward flow. I stayed in this state for a long time, drawing a lot of strength and emotional nourishment from this energy.

4. Out-of-Body Experience

This is a well-documented and very persuasive report of an out-of-body experience, told by Kimberly Clark.

From *The Near-Death Experience*, by B. Greyson and C.P. Flynn. Charles C. Thomas, Chicago, IL: 1984

My first encounter with a near-death experience involved a patient named Maria, a migrant worker who was visiting friends in Seattle and had a severe heart attack. She was brought into the hospital by the rescue squad one night and admitted to the coronary care unit. I got involved in her care as a result of her social and financial problems. A few days after her admission, she had a cardiac arrest. Because she was closely monitored and was otherwise in good health, she was brought back quickly, intubated for a couple of hours to make sure that her oxygenation was adequate, and then extubated.

Later in the day I went to see her, thinking that she might have some anxiety about the fact that her heart had stopped. In fact, she was anxious, but not for that reason. She was in a state of relative agitation, in contrast to her usual calmness. She wanted to talk to me about something. She said: "The strangest thing happened when the doctors and nurses were working on me: I found myself looking down from the ceiling at them working on my body."

I was not impressed at first. I thought that she might know what had been going on in the room, what people were wearing, and who would be there, since she had seen them all day prior to her cardiac arrest. Certainly she was familiar with the equipment by that time. Since hearing is the last sense to go, I reasoned that she could hear everything that was going on, and while I did not think she was consciously making this up, I thought it might have been a confabulation.

She then told me that she had been distracted by something over the emergency room driveway and found herself outside, as if she had "thought herself" over the emergency room driveway and, in just that instant, she was out there. At this point, I was a little more impressed, since she had arrived at night inside an ambulance and would not have known what the emergency room area looked like. However, I reasoned that perhaps at some point in time her bed had been by the window, she had looked outside, and this had been incorporated into the confabulation.

But then Maria proceeded to describe being further distracted by an object on the third floor ledge on the north end of the building. She "thought her way" up there and found herself "eyeball to shoelace" with a tennis shoe, which she asked me to try to find for her. She needed someone else to know that the tennis shoe was really there to validate her out-of-body experience.

With mixed emotions, I went outside and looked up at the ledges but could not see much at all. I went up to the third floor and began going in and out of patients' rooms and looking out their windows, which were so narrow that I had to press my face to the screen just to see the ledge at all. Finally, I found a room where I pressed my face to the glass and looked down and saw the tennis shoe!

My vantage point was very different from what Maria's had to have been for her to notice that the little toe had worn a place in the shoe and that the lace was stuck under the heel and other details about the side of the shoe not visible to me. The only way she would have had such a perspective was if she had been floating right outside and at very close range to the tennis shoe. I retrieved the shoe and brought it back to Maria; it was very concrete evidence for me.

5. Transpersonal Experience

Sometimes people display knowledge they couldn't possibly have acquired in their life. The following is such a story.

Told by Stanislav Grof, from *Beyond the Brain,* Albany, NY: State University of New York Press. 1985, p. 355-356.

Several years ago, we had in one of our five-day workshops a woman – call her Gladys – who for many years had had serious daily attacks of depression. They usually started after four o'clock every morning and lasted several hours. It was extremely difficult for her to mobilize her resources to face the new day.

In the workshop, she participated in a session of holonomic integration. …

Gladys responded to the breathing session with an extraordinary mobilization of body energies, but did not reach a resolution; this situation was quite exceptional in the work we are doing. The next morning the depression came as usual, but was much more profound than at any previous time. Gladys came to the group in a state of great tension, depression and anxiety. It was necessary to change our program for the morning and do experiential work with her without delay.

We asked her to lie down with her eyes closed, breathe faster, listen to music we were playing, and surrender to any experience that wanted to surface. For about fifty minutes Gladys showed violent tremors and other signs of strong psychomotor excitement; she was screaming loudly and fighting invisible enemies. Retrospectively, she reported that this part of her experience involved the reliving of her birth. At a certain point, her screams became more articulate and started to resemble words in an unknown language. We asked her to let the sounds come out in whatever form they took, without intellectually judging them. Her movements suddenly became extremely stylized and emphatic, and she chanted what appeared to be a powerful prayer.

The impact of this event on the group was extremely strong. Without understanding the words, most members of the group felt deeply moved and started crying. When Gladys completed her chant, she quieted down and moved into a state of ecstasy and bliss in which she stayed, entirely motionless, for more than an hour. Retrospectively, she could not explain what had happened and indicated that she had absolutely no idea what language she was using in her chant.

An Argentinean psychoanalyst present in the group recognized that Gladys had chanted in perfect Sephardic, a language he happened to know. He translated her words as: "I am suffering and I will always suffer. I am crying and I will always cry. I am praying and I will always pray." Gladys herself did not speak even modern Spanish, not to say Sephardic, and did not know what Sephardic language was.

6. Precognition

People often have a sense of some future event, good or bad. Sometimes they ignore these feelings, sometimes they act on them, as in the following example.

As told by Dean Radin from *The Conscious Universe,* New York, NY: HarperEdge, 1997. p. 28-29.

Preparing for a hunting trip later in the month, Alex was cleaning a double-action, six-shot revolver. For safety's sake, he normally kept five bullets in the revolver, with the hammer resting on the sixth, empty chamber. He carefully removed the five bullets, cleaned the gun thoroughly, then began to put the bullets back in the pistol. When he arrived at the fifth and final bullet, he unexpectedly got a bad feeling, a distinct sense of dread that had something to do with that bullet.

Alex worried about this odd feeling, because nothing like it had ever happened to him before. He decided to trust his intuition, so he put the bullet aside and positioned the pistol's hammer as usual over the sixth chamber. The chamber next to it, which normally held the fifth bullet, now was also empty.

Two week later, Alex was at the hunting lodge with his fiancée and her parents. That evening, an ugly argument broke out between the parents over their impending divorce. Alex tried to calm them down, but the father, in a violent rage, grabbed Alex's gun, which was in a drawer, and pointed it at his wife. Alex tried to stop the impending disaster by jumping between the gun and the woman, but he was too late – the trigger had already been pulled. For a horrifying split second, Alex knew that he was about to get shot at point-blank range. But instead of a sudden, blazing death, the pistol went "click." The cylinder had revolved to an empty chamber – the very chamber that *would have contained the fifth bullet* if Alex had not set it aside two weeks before.

7. Internal Tumo Heat

Inner heat can be generated with Vajrayana practices, through the subtle bodies. Here is a Westerner's observation of this phenomena in Tibet.

Told by Herbert Benson, from *The Relaxation Response*, Avon Books, Inc., New York, NY. 2000. p. xxxix-xl .

In the 1980s, my teammates and I repeatedly traveled to Northern India and studied Tibetan monks who were living there in exile. There, our team witnessed incredible mind/body feats. Monks, in little clothing, remained alive and well, practicing an advanced form of meditation in temperatures of zero degrees Fahrenheit at altitudes over fifteen thousand feet in the Himalayan mountains.

In another example, the team watched as monks, dressed in nothing but small loincloths, were draped in wet sheets while exposed to near-freezing temperatures. You and I would experience uncontrollable shivering, develop hypothermia, and perhaps die under these circumstances. But because these monks had developed amazing physiologic control over years of practicing this type of heat-producing meditation, they experienced no distress in these conditions. Instead, within minutes, the body temperatures they produced steamed and dried the wet, cold sheets.

8. Spirits

Sometimes people experience forces from "beyond" making demands on them, as Carl Jung did.

From *Memories, Dreams, Reflections,* by Carl Jung, New York, NY: Vintage Books, 1989. p. 189-191.

In 1916 I felt an urge to give shape to something. I was compelled from within, as it were, to formulate and express what might have been said by Philemon. This was how the *Septem Sermones ad Mortuos*[1] with its peculiar language came into being.

It began with a restlessness, but I did not know what it meant or what "they" wanted of me. There was an ominous atmosphere all around me. I had the strange feeling that the air was filled with ghostly entities. Then it was as if my house began to be haunted. My eldest daughter saw a white figure passing through the room. My second daughter, independently of her elder sister, related that twice in the night her blanket had been snatched away; and that same night my nine-year-old son had an anxiety dream. ...

Around five o'clock in the afternoon on Sunday the front doorbell began ringing frantically. It was a bright summer day; the two maids were in the kitchen, from which the open square outside the front door could be seen. Everyone immediately looked to see who was there, but there was no one in sight. I was sitting near the doorbell, and not only heard it but saw it moving. We all simply stared at one another. The atmosphere was thick, believe me! Then I knew that something had to happen. The whole house was filled as if there were a crowd present, crammed full of spirits. They were packed deep right up to the door, and the air was so thick it was scarcely possible to breathe.

---

[1] Privately printed (n.d.) and pseudonymously subtitled "The Seven Sermons to the Dead written by Basilides in Alexandria, the City where the East toucheth the West."

As for myself, I was all a-quiver with the question: "For God's sake, what in the world is this?" Then they cried out in chorus, "We have come back from Jerusalem where we found not what we sought." That is the beginning of the *Septem Sermones*.

Then it began to flow out of me, and in the course of three evenings the thing was written. As soon as I took up the pen, the whole ghostly assemblage evaporated. The room quieted and the atmosphere cleared. The haunting was over.

9. Future Memory

P.M.H. Atwater has coined the term "Future Memory" for experiences where individuals "pre-live" the future, "remember" events that may not occur until years later. She has documented numerous cases. Here is one of her interviews.

P.M.H. Atwater, *Future Memory*, New York, NY: Birch Lane Press. 1996. p. 23.

I was doing the morning dishes when this rush of energy nearly lifted my head off. I suddenly experienced myself at a dinner party that night, saw who would be there, and took part in what happened and what was said. The whole thing was so real, I decided to make no plans for the evening, just to see what might happen. Sure enough, a friend called and began apologizing all over herself for being so tardy, then she asked if I would come to her dinner party that night. I had to muffle laughter as I accepted her invitation. When I arrived at the party, it was a duplicate of what I had already experienced that morning; every conversation, every wave of a hand, repeated what I previously lived through. I'm glad I "attended" the dinner party before it happened so I could be prepared in advance.

10. Communication with the Deceased

Communication with the deceased may be more common than thought. There are numerous occasions in which Emanuel

Swedenborg communicated with the deceased. Here is one of his better-known incidents.

From, *The Presence of Other Worlds*, by Wilson Van Dusen New York, NY: Harper and Row, 1972. p. 142-143.

Queen Louisa Ulrica of Sweden had heard of Swedenborg. She asked Count Scheffer about this man who pretended to talk with the dead. Was he perhaps mad? Count Scheffer knew Swedenborg and replied he was quite sane. He promised to bring him to court. Swedenborg went to court in his nobleman's finery, powdered wig and dress sword. After the queen chatted with foreign ambassadors and other dignitaries, Court Scheffer introduced Swedenborg to her. She asked whether he could really converse with the deceased? He answered yes. She asked if this skill could be learned by others. He said it couldn't, that it was a gift of the lord. After some further conversation, the queen asked him to take a commission to her brother. The queen, the king, Count Scheffer, and Swedenborg adjourned to a quiet spot where the queen gave Swedenborg her message. The queen and her brother had been separated by tragedy because their countries were at war with each other when he died. Afterward they dined at the royal table, where Emanuel patiently answered many questions of the spiritual world. Many observers felt the queen had not really asked anything very serious of Swedenborg because she didn't believe in his powers.

Some time afterward Count Scheffer again brought Swedenborg to court. He met the queen in her White Room surrounded by ladies-in-waiting. She lightly asked if he had a message from her brother. Swedenborg answered yes and suggested that they speak alone, and he related what he had learned from the queen's brother. The queen was variously described as in shock, disturbed, or so indisposed that she had to retire. She said later that Swedenborg had reported what no other living person knew. Swedenborg's servants reported that for days all the great people of the realm came in carriages to learn the queen's secret, but he did not reveal it.

Later a reporter asked the queen of the incident and she affirmed it. The royal person was described as no weak-minded woman. "Nevertheless, she appeared to me so convinced of Swedenborg's supernatural intercourse with spirits, that I scarcely durst venture to intimate any doubts ... and a royal air – 'Je ne suis pas facilement dupee (I am not easily fooled), put an end to all my attempts at refutation."

11. After-Death Communication

Millions of people believe they have had "visitations" from a deceased friend or relative. They all feel it was too real to be a dream, and typically the experiencer feels comforted by the encounter. Rarely are people willing to talk about their experience, for fear of being ridiculed or simply not believed. A typical example is as follows.

From *After Death Communication*, by Louis E. LaGrand, Ph.D., Llewellyn Publications, St. Paul, Minnesota. 1997: p. 183-184.

When I was eighteen years old my closest friend was killed in a car accident. One night after her death she appeared to me as an angel. When it all began I was in a deep sleep. When I realized what was happening I was sitting up in bed with an angel floating over the stairwell. She was beautiful (in a pink dress) and it was Sherry. She was asking me questions about her boyfriend Brian and telling me to talk to him. It all felt so real. I was awake enough to go downstairs and tell my mother. Thank goodness she was supportive and told me it very well could be real. I felt so peaceful when I was talking to her. To this day (I'm thirty-four) it feels like a true experience.

In reality, I feel it was a spiritual experience. I was struggling and grieving so intensely on my own. Sherry's loss for me was just devastating. She was a friend I phoned daily and sat with on the bus and stayed at her house on weekends. I needed to know that she was okay. I felt confused about death. I felt it was her spirit that came to reassure me.

The message I received was that she was OK. She looked beautiful. She had been injured horribly in the accident. Now there were no visible scars on her face. She had looked horrid in the casket and that was so frightening to me. Her angel appearance reassured me that she was okay. I also wanted to talk to her boyfriend but wasn't able to. I was not on good terms with him because he was abusive to her before her death and I didn't like him. Sherry encouraged me to talk to him. I knew he would understand what I was going through too. That experience gave me permission to reach out for help. I cannot recall who I shared the experience with besides my mother – but I did reach out and talk to friends. It was a great help to me.

12. Inner vision

Numerous people have reported an inner vision. Here Jaques Lusseyran describes how he experienced the inner light after losing his sight at the age of eight. During World War II, although blind, he led 600 fellow youths in underground resistance in France.

From *And There Was Light*, by Jacques Lusseyran, Parabola Books, New York, NY: 1999.

Being blind was not at all as I had imagined it. Nor was it as the people around me seemed to think. They told me that to be blind meant not to see. Yet how was I to believe them when I saw? Not at once, I admit. Not in the days immediately after the operation. For at that time I still wanted to use my eyes. I followed their usual path. I looked where I was in the habit of seeing things before the accident, and there was anguish, a lack, a void that filled me with what grown-ups called despair.

Finally, one day, and it was not long in coming, I realized that I was looking in the wrong way. It was as simple as that. I was making something very like the mistake people make who change their glasses without adjusting themselves. I was looking too far off, and too much on the surface of things.

This was much more than a simple discovery; it was a revelation. I can still see myself in the Champ de Mars, where my father took me for a walk a few days after the accident. Of course I knew the garden well, its ponds, its railings, its iron chairs. I even knew some of the trees personally, and naturally I wanted to see them again. But I couldn't. I threw myself forward into the space, which I did not recognize because it no longer held anything familiar to me.

At this point some instinct – I was almost about to say "a hand" – made me change course. I began to look more carefully, not at things but at a world closer to myself, looking from an inner place at one further within, instead of toward the world outside. Immediately, the substance of the universe drew together, redefined and peopled itself anew. I was aware of a radiance emanating from a place I knew nothing about, a place which could just as well have been outside me as within. But the radiance was there, or, to put it more precisely, a light. It was a fact.

I felt indescribable relief and a happiness so great it almost made me laugh. Confidence and gratitude came as if a prayer had been answered. I found light and joy at the same moment, and I can say without hesitation that from that time on light and joy have never been separate in my experience. I have had them or lost them together.

I saw light and went on seeing it, though I was blind. I said so in others' presence, but for many years I think I did not say it very loud. Until I was nearly fourteen, I remember, I called the experience, which kept renewing itself inside me, "my secret," and spoke of it only to my most intimate friends. I don't know whether they believed me or not, but they listened to me, for they were friends. And what I told them had a greater value than being merely true; it had the value of being beautiful, a dream, an enchantment, almost like magic.

The amazing thing was that this was not magic for me at all, but reality. I could no more have denied it than people with eyes can deny that they see. I was not light myself, I knew that, but I bathed in it as in an element. Blindness had suddenly brought light much closer. I could feel it rising, spreading, resting on objects, giving them form, then leaving them –

withdrawing or diminishing is what I mean, for the opposite of light was never present. Sighted people always talk about the night of blindness, and that idea seems to them quite natural. But there was no such night for me. At every waking hour and even in my dreams, I lived in a stream of light.

Without my eyes, I perceived light to be much more stable than it had been before. There were no longer the same differences between things lighted brightly, less brightly, or not at all. I saw the whole world in terms of light, existing through it and because of it. Colors, all the colors of the rainbow, also survived. For me, a child who loved to draw and paint, the colors were an unexpected celebration. I spent hours playing with them, and all the more easily now that they were more docile than they used to be.

13. Levitation

The ability of some eastern meditators to levitate has always intrigued Westerners. But Joseph of Cupertino was such a successful levitator that he became the Patron Saint of Pilots, the Air Force, and Astronauts.

From *Saints Preserve Us,* by Sean Kelly and Rosemary Rogers, Random House, NY: 1993. p. 166-67.

The famous "flying monk" was born in a garden shed because his father, who died soon after his birth, had sold the house to pay off debts. His widowed mother resented her slow, pigeon-toed son, and other children called him "Boccapeerta" ("the Gaper") because his mouth always hung open. Bad-tempered and a failed shoemaker, Joseph was dismissed by the Capuchins and joined the Franciscans as a servant. A lucky break enabled him to become a novice – the exam he was given was based on the only text he was able to read. He became more devout and was so happy to be a priest that he mailed his underwear back to his mother, because his habit was all he needed (he didn't remove it for two years). Soon after he became a priest, his famous levitations began; according to his biographers, Joseph levitated over 100 times. He was able to fly high above the altar and once helped workmen by lifting a huge cross thirty-six feet in the air and then stayed perched on top of the cross for several hours. Fellow friars soon took to flying around on his back. During his flights he would issue shrill cries and afterward would dissolve into fits of laughter. The Spanish ambassador arrived for an interview with the "flying friar," but as soon as Joseph entered the church he spied a statue of Mary (to whom he had a special devotion), and flew over the heads of the Spanish entourage, settled for a while at the foot of the statue, then flew back over the crowd, shrieking, and headed toward his room. Christmas carols were especially moving to him, and as soon as they started, Joseph would fly straight upward in a kneeling position and stay that way until the caroling stopped. Church authorities, disturbed by this phenomenon and accusing him of "drawing crowds after him like a Messiah," placed him in seclusion, actually making him a prisoner. But pilgrims kept finding him, so Joseph was moved from place to place, his notoriety preceding him. The controversy around the Saint, who could also predict the future, caused him to slip into deep melancholia. His last flight was, appropriately enough, on the Feast of the Assumption a month before his death, in 1663.

14. Power of Iconography

In *Visions of Innocence*, Edward Hoffman relates numerous transforming experiences people have had in their childhood. Typically they were unable to relate these events without being laughed at. Hoffman also points out how children are typically regarded as close to the divine. The following is one such story.

From *Visions of Innocence, Spiritual and Inspirational Experiences of Childhood,* by Edward Hoffman, Shambala, Boston, MA: 1992, p. 131-132.

Harvey is a thirty-nine-year-old communications consultant living in suburban Philadelphia. Having grown up

Catholic in New York City, he recalls: "One Sunday, when I was about eight, my father and I visited a Greek Orthodox church, rather than attend our regular Mass. When I entered the unfamiliar building a few blocks from our home, my attention was instantly captivated by a huge Jesus Pantocrator icon. I was enthralled, for it seemed to possess a tremendous force and power.

"Like a great and magnificent rock," Harvey recounts, "the memory of that icon has weighed upon my psyche to this day. Whenever I remember that childhood event, it's always in the form of a wordless watching: a kind of contemplation that thrives in the absence of spoken words.

"Mother Tessa Bielicki has described such contemplation as 'iconic looking,' which provides a long, loving look at the real. In *Behold the Beauty of the Lord: Praying with Icons,* Henri Nouwen explains that icons aren't easy to 'see' or to comprehend immediately. 'It's only gradually, after a patient, prayerful presence that they start speaking to us. And as they speak, they speak more to our inner than our outer senses. They speak to the heart that searches for God.'"

Harvey adds: "This has certainly been true for me. My childhood encounter with the icon of Jesus powerfully ignited my life's spiritual journey. I'm only now realizing that I've passed through several meaningful phases in which God has been present in various ways. I view my present task as recovering these moments as vital and intimate dialogue."

15. Visions

Saints are frequently known for their "visions," and their attempts to explain their visions to the rest of us. Typically they are hesitant to take on their mission suggested by their visions, as was Hildegard of Bingen.

From *Hildegard of Bingen*, by Heinrich Schipperges, Markus Wiener Publishers, Princeton, NJ: 1997. p. 10-11.

At the age of sixteen the novice Hildegard took the veil from the hands of Otto, Bishop of Bamberg. When Jutta died in 1136 Hildegard was elected to head the convent at Dissbodenberg. It was during these years that the young Hildegard had discovered within herself a curious intuitive gift that she called her *visio*, her ability to have visions. She saw such a great light that her soul quaked, though she was unable to communicate it to others.

Hildegard stated emphatically that she had not invented this *visio*. Nor, she said, had any other person devised of affected it. Rather, the meaning of the scriptures revealed itself to her, in visions, or more precisely, in auditory experiences, in the form of an intuitive feeling that instantly abrogated the laws of reason and produced enlightenment. Her intuition, Hildegard went on to explain, saw all things in the light of God through the five senses. The sense of sight perceived lovingly (*amat*), the sense of hearing discerned (*discernit*), the organs of taste savored (*sapit*), those of smell selected (*eligit*), and those of touch took whatever pleased them. "God, the creator of all things, is reflected in our senses." Human beings perceived God through the mirror of faith, just as the Living Light shined into the hearts of men through the same mirror. The external world was but the medium of enlightenment. "God cannot be perceived directly. Rather, he is known through creation, through humankind alone which is a mirror of all God's wonders."

In 1141, shortly after she turned forty, Hildegard had another vision, the real turning point in her career. The spirit of God touched her heart like a burning flame, transforming the silent visionary into a prophetess. The divine call became clearer and clearer. "Say and write what you see and hear!" a voice from above commanded. At first Hildegard was afraid and hesitated to act. She used illness as an escape before summoning the courage to make her visions public.

Plagued by doubts about her mission, Hildegard in 1147 turned to Bernard, the Abbot of Clairvaux, already an influential ecclesiastic, an implored him in a famous letter: "I beg you, Father, that you hear me questioning you!" Thus she began her missive, immediately addressing her concern: "I am much disturbed by a kind of vision that appears to me through the mysteries of the spirit … I wretched and more than wretched in the name of woman, I have looked since childhood on great wonders which my tongue could not speak about if God's spirit had not taught me to believe." Never – "not a single hour" – since her infancy had she lived in certainty. Hence her fervent plea: "So tell me what you think? I have no school knowledge about outside things. Hence my doubts and my uncertainty!" Hildegard was seeking more than consolation and solace; she hoped Bernard would give her some sign of support: "I have placed myself in your soul that you may counsel me whether you think I should tell everything publicly or remain silent!" In conclusion, she beseeched Bernard not to remain indifferent, but to answer her as someone who had a reputation as a valiant fighter: "For you uplift not only yourself, but the world, to the good of all. You are an eagle looking directly at the sun!" …

St. Bernard's efforts were among the more important reasons for this humble nun becoming a *prophetissa teutonica*.

16. Process Therapy

Body symptoms can represent something that we have repressed, or new things we need to learn about. The following is an example told by Arnold Mindell in his work, about a little girl medically diagnosed with skin cancer (melanoma).

As told by Arnold Mindell from *Your Body Speaks its Dreams*, on New Dimensions Foundation radio.

I saw a little girl with a melanoma between her eyes. A melanoma is a black piece of skin cancer. It is usually rapidly consuming the person. A little tiny piece between her eyes. She didn't realize that it could be terminal – she thought it was a little black thing. So I said, "It is just what you think it is, a little black thing." She said, "Well, what does that mean?" I said, "Well, look at yourself in the mirror." She looked in the mirror and saw this little black thing between her eyes, and she said, "Well Dr. Mindell I can tell you what that is." I said, "What is it?" She said, "That's an eye." So I said "Well, let's draw an eye right on your face there." We drew her third eye. And then I said, "Now, use it, open it up." She opened up her third eye, and I said, "What do you see?" She said, "Oh, I see all sorts of things," and she developed a mediumistic character. She hadn't known that she was a medium before. Her melanoma went away as she became a medium. I couldn't say that she had been repressing being a medium before; she was only five or six [years old]. So there's an example of information that came up that she never knew about. ...

We told them [the Medical Doctors] not to cut that [melanoma], to leave it be. There was a big scene. "Well you can't do that with melanoma. That will be the end of her." But I said, "No, with people who are ready to integrate stuff so quickly, don't worry about it. That's going to go away by itself. That's all about integration."

17. Astrology

Although most Western scientists or physicians do not take astrology seriously today, we find that in the 17th Century, Renaissance man, Robert Fludd, believed that a doctor ignorant of astrology was no more than a quack. Here is a short anecdote told by Robert Fludd.

From *Robert Fludd*, by Joscelyn Godwin, Shambhala Publications, Boulder, CO: 1979. p. 6.

While I was working on my music treatise, I scarcely left my room for a week on end. One Tuesday a young man from Magdalen came to see me, and dined in my room. The following Sunday I was invited to dine with a friend from the town, and while dressing for the occasion I could not find my valuable sword-belt and scabbard, worth ten French gold pieces. I asked everyone in the college if they knew anything about it, but with no success. I therefore drew up a horary chart for the moment at which I had noticed the loss, and deduced from the position of Mercury and other features that the thief was a talkative youth situated in the East, while the stolen goods must now be in the South.

On thinking this over I remembered my guest of Tuesday, whose college lay directly to the east of St. John's. I sent my servant to approach him politely, but he swore that he had touched nothing of mine. Next I sent my servant to speak to the boy who had accompanied my visitor on that day, and with harsh words and threats he made him confess that he had stolen the goods and taken them to a place I knew near Christ Church where people listened to music and consorted women. This confirmed my conjecture that the place was to the south of St. John's, and since Mercury had been in the house of Venus, that accorded with the association with music and women. After this the boy was taken into the presence of his companion and flung to the ground. He swore that he had indeed committed the crime, and begged my servant to say no more: he promised to retrieve the belt and scabbard on the following day. This was done, and I received my stolen property wrapped in two beautiful parchments. It emerged that the music-house near Christ Church was the lair of a receiver of stolen goods who had robbed many degenerate scholars, wasting them with gluttony and womanizing. My friend implored me to desist from the study of astrology, saying that I could not have solved this crime without demonic aid. I thanked him for his advice.

18. Life Review

The following story demonstrates how one's life can "flash" before one's eyes, but it also shows the importance of understanding that our existence extends beyond our birth and death.

From *Beyond Death,* by Stanislav and Christina Grof, Thames and Hudson, London, England: 1980. p. 10-11.

During the several seconds that my car was in motion, I had an experience that seemed to span centuries. I rapidly moved from sheer terror and overwhelming fear for my life to a profound knowledge that I would die. Ironically with that knowledge came the deepest sense of peace and serenity that I have ever encountered. It was as though I had moved from the periphery of my being – the body that contained me – to the very centre of myself, a place that was imperturbable, totally quiet and at rest. The mantra that I had previously been using in meditation sprang into my consciousness and revolved automatically, with an ease I had never before known. Time seemed to have disappeared as I watched sequences from my life passing before me like a movie, quite rapidly, but with amazing detail. When I reached the point of death, it seemed that I was facing an opaque curtain of some kind. The momentum of the experience carried me, still completely calm, through the curtain and I realized that it had not been a point of termination, but rather of transition. The only way that I can describe the next sensation is to say that every part of my, whatever I was at that moment, felt without question a far-reaching and encompassing continuum beyond what I had previously thought of as death. It was as though the force that had moved me toward death and then past it would endlessly continue to carry me, through ever-expanding vistas.

It was at this point that my car hit a truck with great impact. As it came to rest, I looked around and realized that by some miracle I was still alive. And then, an amazing thing happened. As I sat in the midst of the tangled metal, I felt my individual boundaries begin to melt. I started to merge with everything around me – with the policemen, the wreck, the workers with crowbars trying to liberate me, the ambulance, the flowers on a nearby hedge, and the television cameramen. Somewhere, I could see and feel my injuries, but they did not seem to have anything to do with me; they were merely part of a rapidly expanding network that included much more than my body. The sunlight was unusually bright and golden and the entire world seemed to shimmer with a beautiful radiance. I felt blissful and exuberant, even in the middle of the drama around me, and I remained in that state for several days in the hospital. The accident and the experience that accompanied it totally transformed my world-view and my way of understanding existence. Previously, I had not had much interest in spiritual areas and my concept of life was that it was contained between birth and death. The thought of death had always frightened me. I had believed that "we walk across life's stage but once," and then – nothing. Consequently I had been driven by the fear that I would not have a chance to do all that I wanted to accomplish during my life. Now, the world and my place in it feel completely different. I feel that my self-definition transcends the notion of a limited physical body existing in a limited time frame. I know myself to be part of a larger, unrestricted, creative network that could be described as divine.

19. Thought Transfer

Can thoughts be transferred directly from one individual to another? The following was told to me in a personal communication.

A group of friends gathered together on a weekly basis to explore psychic phenomena. The center of our group was a well-known psychic. One evening we were sitting on the floor in a circle with people from this group, just talking. For some reason I wasn't in the mood to carry on a discussion, and the person on my right was asking me questions he was interested in. I responded to his inquiries, but for some reason I really didn't feel like talking. At one point when he asked me a question I did not answer verbally. As the thought formed in my head and I was about to speak, I hesitated, and instead of speaking, the thought seemed to eject out of the right side of my head, and I noticed a sensation on the right side of my head, and a "flash" directed toward the person I was speaking with. I would not have paid much attention to it, but the person sitting across from us said, "Did you see that? A light just shot out of his head." Several other people in the circle had noticed as well. The person on my right was continuing to ask questions as if I had responded verbally to him. He said he thought that I had answered him, and was continuing with the conversation. I had no idea how this process took place and could not repeat it if I tried, although I have never seriously tried.

20. Qigong

The following information was taken from an article written by Chiu-Nan Lai from East West Journal, 1983, entitled *Ch'i Gong; Chinese Cancer Patients Exercise Their Way Back to Health.*

Madame Guo Lin of Beijing, was raised by her grandfather and started learning Taoist practices and qigong at the age of six. As a painter of traditional Chinese style, her work took her to the mountains where she met many qigong masters who enriched her knowledge of this ancient art. Madame Guo Lin first utilized qigong as a cancer treatment when she developed cancer of the uterus. Doctors, both Western and traditional Chinese, said they could do nothing more for her. She decided to be her own doctor, and began modifying traditional qigong to suit her case, and kept practicing it. Her skill improved and so did her health. Her "untreatable" cancer went into remission. She began to teach qigong in her free time in Beijing's big parks during the Cultural Revolution. She had a real hard time because she was labeled a 'swindler' and had to move from place to place because qigong was banned as a superstition. She did not give in. Her daughter, living in California, encouraged her to come to the United States, but she could not leave her patients. The story is told that she would be incarcerated and her patients would demand her release.

Madame Guo Lin persisted and personally supervised qigong classes at the Purple Bamboo Garden Park with the help of dozens of volunteer teaching assistants. Many universities, government institutions and army units invited her to give lectures, for which she charged nothing. "My purpose is to popularize qigong and rescue the dying," she said. In response to this revival of interest in qigong, Madame Guo Lin published a number of books, including the *New Qigong Therapy (Books I and II), and New Qigong Therapy for Cancer Treatment and Prevention.* Madame Guo has no doubts. "From my own experience I know that qigong has opened up a way for those who cannot undergo surgical operation. It also reduces the side-effects of chemotherapy and radiation treatment."

21. Universal Consciousness

A person can have an experience that puts him in touch with Universal Consciousness, and he will relate the experience in the best way he can. Metaphors must be used to express ideas unfamiliar to our ordinary experience of this world. The following is such an account.

Anonymously told, from *The Adventure of Self-Discovery,* by Stanislav Grof, Albany, NY: State University of New York Press. 1988, p. 144.

I suddenly understood the principle underlying the organization of the cosmos. It was the Universal Consciousness playing out an endless series of dramas in a way we can see represented on the theater stage or in the movies. In this drama it plays a game of losing itself for the purpose of finding itself again. The Universal Consciousness would plunge into separation, rejection, pain, evil, agony, and darkness to experience the infinite joy of rediscovering its original pristine, safe, and blissful state. Its true identity is indivisible oneness, beyond negativity and dualities of any kind. To make the journey, it had to create the illusion of space, matter, and time and, together with it, the categories of evil, darkness, pain and destruction.

I continued to think about the analogy to the movies; it seemed particularly fitting as a metaphor for the process of creation. ... A single source of light creating an infinite number of pictures and scenes projected on the screen! It is also possible to follow the beam of light all the way into the interior of the projector. There is the emptiness from which the light comes. The film itself then would be an equivalent of the archetypes determining the type of experiences created by projection as a four-dimensional space-time continuum.

Bibliography

1. Binder, P. *Magic Symbols of the World*. UK: Hamlyn Publishing Group, 1972
2. Blofeld, J. *Mantra: Sacred Words of Power*. New York, NY: E.P. Dutton & Co., 1977
3. Bowman, C. *Children's Past Lives: How Past Life Memories Affect Your Child*. New York, NY: Bantam Books, 1998
4. Campbell, J. *The Hero with A Thousand Faces*. New York, NY: Bollinger Foundation, 1973
5. Campbell, J. *The Masks of God: Creative Mythology*. New York, NY: Viking Press,
6. Campbell, D. *The Mozart Effect: Tapping The Power Of Music To Heal The Body, Strengthen The Mind And Unlock The Creative Spirit*. New York, NY: HarperTrade, 2001.
7. Dossey, L. Healing, *Energy & Consciousness: Into the Future or a Retreat to the Past?*: Journal of Subtle Energies, 1994:5
8. Dossey, L. *Healing Words, The Power of Prayer and the Practice of Medicine*. San Francisco, CA: HarperSanFrancisco; 1993
9. Eliade, M. *Myth and Reality*. New York, NY: Harper Colophon Books; 1975
10. Eliade, M. *Myths, Rites, Symbols*. New York, NY: Harper and Row; 1976
11. Eliade, M. *Rites and Symbols of Initiation*. New York, NY: Harper and Row; 1965
12. Govinda, A. *Foundations of Tibetan Mysticism*. New York, NY: Samuel Wiser; 1974:147.
13. Grof, S. *Beyond the Brain*. New York, NY: State University of New York Press; 1985
14. Grof, S. *The Adventure of Self-Discovery: Dimensions of Consciousness and New Perspectives in Psychotherapy and Inner Exploration*. New York, NY: State University of New York Press; 1988
15. Hawking, S.W. *A Brief History of Time,* New York, NY: Bantam Books; 1988
16. Jung, C.G. *The Meaning of Psychology for Modern Man: Civilization in Transition*, 1933

17. Jung, C.G. *Mysterium Coniunctionis*, Princeton, NJ: Princeton University Press; 1977

18. Kazanis, D. *The Physical Basis for Subtle Bodies and the Near-Death Experience*, The Journal of Near-Death Experiences; Winter, 1995:101-116.

19. Kuhn, T.S. *The Structure of Scientific Revolutions.* Chicago IL: University of Chicago Press, 1962

20. Leadbeater, C.W. *Man Visible and Invisible.* Wheaton, IL: The Theosophical Publishing House; 1987:10.

21. Lovelock, J.E. *Gaia: A New Look at Life on Earth.* Oxford, England: Oxford University Press; 1987

22. Michell, J. *The Earth Spirit, Its Ways, Shrines and Mysteries.* New York, NY: Avon Books; 1975

23. Mindell, A. *Dreambody.* Boston, MA: Sigo Press, 1982

24. Mookerjee, A. *Kundalini.* Rochester, VT: Destiny Books; 1991

25. O'Connor, F. *The Complete Short Stories.* New York, NY: Farrar, Straus and Giroux; 1971

26. Ponce, C. *Kabbalah: An Introduction and Illumination for the World.* San Francisco, CA: Straight Arrow Books. 1973,

27. Read, H. *The Forms of Things Unknown.* Cleveland, OH: The World Publishing Company. 1967.

28. Richards, M.C. *Toward Wholeness: Rudolf Steiner Education in America.* Middletown, CT: Wesleyan University Press; 1980

29. Radin, D. *The Conscious Universe.* San Francisco, CA: HarperEdge, 1997

30. Rinpoche, C. T. *Cutting Through Spiritual Materialism.* Berkeley, CA: Shambala Publications; 1973

31. Rinpoche, C. T. *The Myth of Freedom and the Way of Meditation.* Berkeley, CA: Shambala Publications, 1976.

32. Rinpoche, S. *The Tibetan Book of Living and Dying.* San Francisco, CA: HarperSanFrancisco, 1992: 98.

33. Schrödinger, E. *My View of the World.* Cambridge, MA: Cambridge University Press, 1964

34. Schrödinger, E. *What is Life?* Cambridge, MA: Cambridge University Press; 1947

35. Sheldrake, R. *The Presence of the Past.* Rochester, VT: Park Street Press, 1995

36. Shroder, T. *Old Souls: Compelling Evidence from Children Who Remember Past Lives*. New York, NY. Simon & Schuster, 1999

37. Smith, F.F. *Inner Bridges: A Guide to Energy Movement and Body Structure*. Atlanta, GA: Humanics New Age; 1986

38. Stevenson, I. *Children Who Remember Previous Lives*. Charlottesville, VA: University Press of Virginia; 1987

39. Tammet, D. *Born on a Blue Day*. New York, NY: Free PressA Division of Simon & Schuster, Inc.; 2006

40. Tansley, D.V. *The Subtle Body*. New York, NY: Thames and Hudson, Inc.; 1984:80.

41. Tompkins, P. and C. Bird. *The Secret Life of Plants*. New York, NY: Harper and Row. 1989

42. Trefil, J. *Dark Matter*. Smithsonian, 1993

43. Van Dusen, W. *The Presence of Other Worlds*. New York, NY: Harper and Row, 1974

44. Wilber, K. *Quantum Questions*. Boulder, CO: Shambala Publications, 1984

45. Wilber, K. *The Marriage of Sense and Soul: Integrating Science and Religion*. New York, NY: Random House; 1998

In the beginning was God,
Today is God,
Tomorrow will be God.
Who can make an image of God?
He has no body.
He is a word which comes out of your mouth.
That word! It is no more,
It is past, and still it lives!
So is God.

– Pygmy Hymn

Footnotes

---

[1] Alice A. Bailey and D. Khul. *The Soul, The Quality of Life*. New York, NY: Lucis Publishing Company. 1990 pp. 20-22.

[2] Kazanis, Deno. "The Physical Basis for Subtle Bodies and the Near-Death Experience," The Journal of Near-Death Studies (Winter, 1995)

[3] Anagarika Govinda. *Foundations of Tibetan Mysticism*. New York: Samuel Wiser; 1974, p. 147.

[4] David V. Tansley. *The Subtle Body*. New York, NY: Thames and Hudson; 1984, p. 5

[5] Anagarika Govinda, *Foundations of Tibetan Mysticism*. New York, NY: Samuel Wiser; 1974, p. 148.

[6] Ibid.

[7] Ibid., p.149

[8] Ibid., p. 135

[9] Fritz F. Smith. *Inner Bridges: A Guide to Energy Movement and Body Structure*. Atlanta, GA: Humanics New Age; 1986, p. 50.

[10] S. Grof, *The Adventure of Self-Discovery*, Albany, NY: State University of New York Press; 1988, p. 115

[11] James Trefil, "Dark Matter," Smithsonian (June, 1993), p. 27

[12] Ibid., p. 27-29

[13] C. W. Leadbeater, *Man Visible and Invisible*. Wheaton, IL: Theosophical Publishing House; 1987, p.10.

[14] Ibid.

[15] L. Dossey, "Energy and Consciousness: Into the Future or a Retreat to the Past?" Journal of Subtle Energies (1994), P.5

[16] David V. Tansley, *The Subtle Body*. New York, NY: Thames and Hudson: 1984, p. 23

[17] S. Grof, *The Adventure of Self-Discovery*. Albany, NY: State University of New York Press: 1988, p. 111

[18] Ajit Mookerjee, *Kundalini*. Rochester, VT: Destiny Books; 1991, p.71

[19] L. Dossey, *Healing Words*, The Power of Prayer and the Practice of Medicine. San Francisco, CA: Harper SanFrancisco; 1993, P. 198

[20] Benson, H., and M. Epstein. The Placebo Effect: a Neglected Asset in the Care of Patients. JAMA 232:1225-1227, 1975.

[21] Wayne Jonas. Exploring the State of the Art; Presented at the Conference of the Institute of the Noetic Sciences, 1996.

[22] Peter Tompkins and Christopher Bird. *The Secret Life of Plants*. New York, NY: Harper and Row; 1989, p. 11

[23] Paul Smith. www.rvconference.org

[24] C.W. Leadbeater, *Man Visible and Invisible*. Wheaton, IL: Theosophical Publishing House; 1987, p.11

[25] Mircea Eliade, *Myths, Dreams and Mysteries*. London, England: Collins; 1968, P. 90

[26] Felicitas D. Goodman: *Where the Spirits Ride the Wind*. Bloomington, IN: Indiana University Press. 1990, P. 89

[27] Pearl Binder. *Magic Symbols of the World*. UK: Hamlyn Publishing Group, Inc. : 1972, p. 74-75

[28] Barbara Harris, *Spiritual Awakenings*, Baltimore, MD: Stage 3 Books; 1993, p. 17

[29] Kwasi Wiredu, African Studies Quarterly, The Online Journal of African Studies www.africa.ufl.edu.

[30] Ibid.

[31] Carol Bowman, *Children's Past Lives: How Past Life Memories Affect Your Child*. New York NY: Batam Books, 1998, p. 123-124.

[32] Ibid. , p. 124

[33] Sogyam Rinpoche, *The Tibetan Book of Living and Dying*. San Francisco CA: Harper SanFrancisco, 1992, p. 98

[34] Daniel Tammet, *Born on a Blue Day*, New York, NY: Free Press, A Division of Simon & Schuster, Inc.; 2006, p.3-5

[35] Rupert Sheldrake, *The Presence of the Past: Morphic Resonance and the Habits of Nature*. Rochester, VA: Park Street Press; 1995, p.102

[36] John Michell. *The Earth Spirit, Its Ways, Shrines and Mysteries*. New York, NY: Avon Books; 1975, p.4

[37] Ibid.

[38] James E. Lovelock. *Gaia: A New Look at Life on Earth*. Oxford, England: Oxford University Press; 1987.

[39] John Michell. *The Earth Spirit, Its Ways, Shrines and Mysteries*. New York, NY: Avon Books; 1975, p.12

[40] "Teilhard de Chardin, Pierre," Microsoft® Encarta® Online Encyclopedia 2001 http://encarta.msn.com © 1997-2001 Microsoft

[41] James Trefil, "Dark Matter," Smithsonian (June, 1993) p.34

[42] James Joyce, *Finnegans Wake*, New York NY: The Viking Press; 1982, p.3

[43] Ed Friedlander, M.D., *Understanding William Blake's "The Tyger,"* Internet.

[44] Ken Wilber, *The Marriage of Sense and Soul*. New York, NY: Random House; 1998, p.37

[45] Ibid., p. 38-39

[46] Ervin Laszlo, *Science and the Akashic Field*, Rochester, VT: Inner Traditions, 2004, p. 142.

[47] Ervin Laszlo, *Science and the Akashic Field*, Rochester, VT: Inner Traditions, 2004, p. 141.
[48] David Tansley, *Subtle Bodies*, New York, NY: Thames and Hudson; 1984, p. 8
[49] Carl G. Jung, *Dreams*, Translated by R.F.C. Hull, Princeton, NJ: Princeton University Press. 1974, p.3
[50] Wilson Van Dusen, *The Presence of Other Worlds, The Findings of Emanuel Swedenborg*. New York, NY: Harper & Row; 1974
[51] Carl G. Jung, *The Meaning of Psychology for Modern Man: Civilization in Transition,* 1933, P. 304
[52] Arnold Mindell in an Interview with The Monthly Aspectarian.
[53] Ibid.
[54] Joseph Campbell, Videotape Series of Lectures
[55] Ibid.
[56] Mircea Eliade, *Myth and Reality*. New York, NY: Harper Colophon Books; 1975, p.1
[57] Joseph Campbell. *The Hero with a Thousand Faces*. Princeton, NJ: Princeton University Press; 1973, p.3
[58] "Mudra." Microsoft Encarta Encyclopedia 2001. 1993-2000 Microsoft Corporation.
[59] Felicitas D. Goodman: *Where the Spirits Ride the Wind*. Bloomington, IN: Indiana University Press. 1990
[60] Barbara Kazanis, On Finding and Respecting Our Own Ways of Grieving, in *Creation Spirituality*, Nov./Dec., 1991.
[61] Charles Ponce. *Kabbalah: An Introduction and Illumination for the World*. San Francisco, CA: Straight Arrow Books. 1973, p.13
[62] Carl G. Jung, *Mysterium Coniunctionis*, Princeton, NJ: Princeton University Press; 1977, p. xiii
[63] Ibid.
[64] Lama Anagarika Govinda, *Foundations of Tibetan Mysticism*. New York, NY: Samuel Weiser; 1974, p. 213
[65] Nikos Kazantzakis, *Zorba the Greek,* New York, NY: Simon and Shuster, p.286
[66] Ibid., p. 291
[67] John Blofeld, *Mantras: Sacred Words of Power*, New York, NY: E.P. Dutton & Co.; 1977, p.39
[68] Ibid.
[69] Ibid.
[70] Stanislav Grof. *The Adventure of Self-Discovery: Dimensions of Consciousness and New Perspectives in Psychology and Inner Exploration.* New York, NY: State university of New York Press; 1988, p.184

71 Don Campbell, *Music and Miracles*. Wheaton IL: Quest Books, 1992, p. 1
72 Mary Carolyn Richards, *Toward Wholeness: Rudolf Steiner Education in America*. Middletown, CT: Wesleyan University Press. 1980, p. 94
73 Barbara Kazanis, "The Arts are Basic," New England Art Ed. Association Conference, 1977
74 Peter Coveney and Roger Highfield, "The Arrow of Time," Flamingo, London 1991, p. 67
75 Bob Edwards, on National Public Radio in an interview with Francis Crick concerning his book "The Astonishing Hypothesis"
76 Thomas Kuhn, *The Structure of Scientific Revolution*. Chicago, IL: The University of Chicago Press, 1965
77 Erwin Schrödinger, *My View of the World*. Cambridge, MA: Cambridge University Press, 1964
78 Ibid.
79 Stanislav Grof. *The Adventure of Self-Discovery: Dimensions of Consciousness and New Perspectives in Psychology and Inner Exploration*. New York, NY: State university of New York Press; 1988, p.160-161.
80 Kazanis, Deno. "The Physical Basis for Subtle Bodies and the Near-Death Experience," The Journal of Near-Death Studies (Winter, 1995), p. 114.
81 John S. Mbiti, *African Religions and Philosophy*. Portsmouth, NH: Heinemann; 1990, p. 74
82 Stanislav Grof, *The Adventure of Self-Discovery*, State University of New York Press, p. 269.
83 Stephen Hawking, *A Brief History of Time*. New York, NY: Bantam Books, 1988, p. 139
84 Edwin Schrödinger, *What is Life?* Cambridge, MA: Cambridge University Press, 1947

www.ingramcontent.com/pod-product-compliance
Lightning Source LLC
LaVergne TN
LVHW051303080426
835509LV00020B/3133